What Christian Leaders
Are Saying About This Book

"In this new book, Eddie and Alice Smith share the importance of harmony between the ministries of church leaders and intercessors. I believe every Christian leader and praying Christian will find this book helpful in fulfilling the Great Commission of our Lord."

Pat Robertson
Chief Executive Officer
The Christian Broadcasting Network

"For years I have thought that if I were Satan, a top priority would be to keep pastors and intercessors apart. That is why I know that Eddie and Alice's new book will definitely frustrate the devil and open new doors for the power of God to flow through our churches and into our communities."

C. Peter Wagner
Chancellor
Wagner Leadership Institute

"This is a book that many of us have been waiting for. I believe that the linking of the ministries of the pastor and intercessor is vitally important for the advancement of our Lord's Kingdom. Eddie and Alice are wonderfully prepared to communicate about this subject since they have modeled what they have written about."

Paul Cedar
Chief Executive Officer
Mission America

"As I read through this book my heart was deeply touched by the truth and clarity in each chapter. Key issues that have kept pastors and intercessors apart were dealt with in integrity. Satan is the accuser of the brethren and the responsible one for much division. I gleaned insight from every page and have a determined fervency to pray for my pastor as well as spiritual leaders across our land. There is a story of a 4th Century Garden Saint of Asia Minor named Phocas that will challenge the depth of your being. I heartily recommend this book to you."

Bobbye Byerly
Prayer Coordinator
World Prayer Center

"This is a remarkable book. God is going to use it to bring healing between intercessors and pastors that I have longed for. For pastors who are frustrated with their intercessors, this book is for you. Intercessors, this is a valuable tool to know how to be the best prayer partner your pastor ever had."

Dr. Cindy Jacobs
Cofounder
Generals of Intercession

"Eddie and Alice Smith candidly address the devastating problem of disunity and improper relationships between intercessors and pastors. They skillfully combine strong exhortation with practical suggestions, seasoned with inspiring illustrations of incredible victories through prayer. I recommend this book to anyone interested in prayer, pray-ERs, and praying."

Larry L. Lewis
National Facilitator for *Celebrate Jesus 2000*
Mission America

"In the Word the Lord has a clear order for victory. He also has a sound foundation declared in Ephesians 4:11. When these gifts align properly we are assured to have his mind over our families, lives, churches, and cities. One key relationship is that between intercessors and pastors, intercessors pave the way for pastors to execute God's vision. Therefore, there must be a good working relationship between these two gifts. This book will help you in seeing the partnership necessary to 'watch after' God's purposes in your region."

Chuck Pierce
World Prayer Center

"Pastors and intercessors around the world are discovering their need for each other and are asking important questions as they pursue their roles and this new relationship. As a pastor and an intercessor, Eddie and Alice have worked closely together. They speak to us from personal experience. We need their wisdom and warnings. I am thankful for a book that is both biblical, practical and essential if this new partnership is to mature and bless the church."

Phil Miglioratti
National Pastors' Prayer Network

"I can't think of two better experienced and qualified people to write a book on this subject! There are many resources available on intercession and spiritual warfare, but none address the often misunderstood relationship between a pastor and his intercessors so thoroughly as this one!"

Paul Tan
Senior Pastor, *Int'l & Indonesian Full Gospel Fellowship*
Claremont, CA
Coordinator, *U.S. Spiritual Warfare Network's Asian Task Force*

"This is an essential book at this strategic time in history. Pastors and intercessors are becoming more aware of the necessity to work closer together. The Smiths provide powerful insight and wisdom for the successful functioning of these teams. I highly recommend this dynamic book as a fundamental tool for those who desire to see transformation come to their cities and territories!"

Barbara Wentroble
President, *Wentroble Ministries*
Author: *Prophetic Intercession* and *A People of Destiny*

"This book has opened my eyes and answered those little nagging questions. I suddenly realize that many of the problems between intercessors and pastors are the result of misunderstandings. What some pastors have seen as people in rebellion has been, in many cases, misguided, poorly taught, over zealous, and inexperienced intercessors who could have and should have been a support and an asset to their pastor and church."

Ace Clarke
Senior Pastor, *The Joshua Center*
Hamilton, Ontario, Canada

"The most rewarding part of this book for me is the clarity with which Eddie and Alice so adequately explain first, what is expected of watchmen (intercessors) and gatekeepers (pastors); and secondly, how effective ministry to a city can be when these roles are understood by each and how they work together."

Joyce James, Th.S.
Prophetic Intercessor

INTERCESSORS & PASTORS

The Emerging Partnership of
of
Watchmen & Gatekeepers

Eddie & Alice
Smith

SpiriTruth Publishing
7710-T Cherry Park Drive, PMB 224
Houston, TX 77095

Phone: (713) 466-4009
Fax: (713) 466-5633
Email: usprayertrack@cs.com
Web: www.usprayertrack.org

Mark Williamson, Editor
Eddie Smith, Cover and Interior Design

Lovingly dedicated to
the pastors and intercessors
with whom we have served.
Your lives of commitment to Christ
continue to shape ours.

INTERCESSORS & PASTORS
The Emerging Partnership of Watchmen & Gatekeepers

- Contents -

Foreword

Dear Intercessor,

The working relationships between intercessors and their pastors vary. Your pastor is a unique individual with his own personality, spiritual gifts, goals and convictions. He will not approach things the same way we do.

Don't attempt to impose the ideas in this book, or your own ideas for that matter, on your pastor. Love him and serve him. Receive your pastor as a gift from God. An excellent prayer guide to use is *Praying God's Will for My Pastor* by Lee Roberts. Praying the Scripture is always uplifting, edifying and credible. Successful, mature relationships are built upon the knowledge of our common human frailty. The only way we can truly know each other is through open communication.

Seek to understand your pastor. Make a personal appointment with him and inquire as to how your ministry of prayer can assist him. Try to understand your pastor's vision for the church, and what, if anything, you can do to partner with him to see it fulfilled.

God will bless your effort. Your prayers will be answered!

Sincerely,
Eddie & Alice
U.S. PRAYER TRACK

Dear Pastor,

We have written much of this book with you in mind. A worldwide explosion of prayer is occurring today. Intercessory prayer has likely become a higher priority in your own life and in the life of your church in recent years. These are exciting and challenging times and we want to help you partner with the people of prayer God has given you.

God is reforming the church into a house of prayer. This is critical to the completion of the Great Commission and the extension of his Kingdom throughout the earth.

Jesus, our example, only did what he saw the Father doing (see John 5:19). If we operate as he did, we must facilitate this reformation. It involves more than adding a prayer meeting, building a prayer room, or developing a prayer ministry. To become a house of prayer the church will have to actually accept a new identity. Are you willing?

This will mean that prayer will permeate every facet of church life, family life, and individual lives. It will mean teaching the entire church to pray. But it will also mean identifying and establishing meaningful ministry partnerships with the pray-ers (intercessors) in your church.

For the past 150 years, American pastors have typically established ministry partnerships with those members who had influence with men. Today they are beginning to understand the need to partner closely with those who have influence with God (see 1 Corinthians 12:21-24).

We offer this book with the hope that it will assist you in understanding and unleashing these unique, closeted prayer ministers. Intercessors will be your greatest blessing and more than likely, your greatest challenge!

Sincerely,
Eddie & Alice
U.S. PRAYER TRACK

CHAPTER ONE

Let the Healing Begin

It was mid-afternoon on May 8, 1998 at the Light the Nations Conference in the Dallas, Texas Convention Center. The atmosphere was heavenly as nearly seven thousand pastors and church leaders finished singing the beautiful worship chorus, *Higher Ground.* Then noted Argentine/American revivalist Edgardo Silvoso invited to the platform author and experienced intercessor Barbara Wentroble, and pastor for more than 30 years, Rich Marshall.

Silvoso described the divisions that have crippled the church through the years, especially the division between pastors and intercessors. It was now time for repentance and forgiveness to begin. The following is a transcript of what was said. This encounter was completely unscripted and impromptu, as the Holy Spirit led them to speak.

A Pastor Repents

Speaking on behalf of the pastors, Rich looked into Barbara's eyes and said sincerely,

> "Barbara, I speak to you personally, but I also speak to you as a representative of all the intercessors. And while I speak to you personally, I also speak to you on behalf of all the pastors, knowing even as I say this that not all the pastors will understand, but we speak as one unit today.
>
> In the past we have taken what God never gave to us . . . control. And we have

thought that because we are called of God, that that gave us some kind of power over the people in the church. That was so wrong. We have not honored the intercessors . . . We have not given you 'place' in the church. We have relegated you to back rooms. And, we have wounded you. We have not listened to you . . . You have brought the word of the Lord to us and we have laughed, and called you strange. We've said, 'that's just the intercessors.'"

With a broken heart, Pastor Rich then knelt at Barbara's feet and continued.

"Barbara, I repent today . . . I kneel before you to ask you to forgive me. It is a new day for the church. It's a new day for me. It's a new day for you. It's a new day for pastors and intercessors. We have just begun to see what can happen when the intercessors are released in all their power. And today we honor you intercessors . . . and we elevate you. Not above what God would elevate you, but we lift you to the place God has given to you. And we declare today . . . and I say to you right now, 'I am sorry. I have sinned against you. Forgive me for wounding you . . . Forgive me for not listening to you . . . Forgive me for the division that came, not just between pastors and intercessors, but the whole clergy/laity division. It is so out of the will of God. And today my sister we are one. And I bless you in the name of the Lord Jesus. Forgive our sin . . . Forgive my sin . . . Forgive my sin.'"

Except for the sobbing of the many intercessors who were deeply touched by Pastor Rich's humble repentance, a holy hush had fallen over the thousands of people in attendance.

An Intercessor Responds

Then Barbara gracefully knelt before Pastor Rich and tearfully responded,

> "Pastor Rich, for myself personally and corporately from the intercessors, we forgive. We forgive. We forgive. As intercessors, we ask you pastors to forgive us. We've thought we were the spiritual ones. There's been pride . . . There's been control . . . For getting out of the timing of God. For . . . trying to get the pastor to do what we thought God was speaking. We ask for forgiveness. We ask you to forgive us for having our own vision and not seeing our place as one that would help the pastor bring forth his vision that God had given him. For not seeing ourselves as servants the Lord had sent to serve the pastor and to serve the leadership. We ask you to forgive us. We ask you to forgive our impure motives of wanting to gather those around us, rather than to see our role as to help bring forth the gathering unto the Lord. We ask you to forgive us today. We ask you to forgive us for not being sensitive to the times when you've been in a hard place, and had a need in your own life. For not being the Aarons and the Hurs who would lift up your hands in the day of battle. Forgive us for walking away from our

assigned posts as your Aarons and Hurs. We ask you to forgive us today.

And we desire this day to take our place as servants that would serve from a pure heart. We ask you to allow us to walk in a covenant relationship with you that God would so join our hearts, even as he joined Jonathan and David, that from this day forward we might be a support and strength to you."

The Pastor Responds

Pastor Rich responded,

"Barbara, we do forgive you. We declare that it is a wonderful day when we can join together as God intended the body of Christ to be. Pastors, as you are now on your knees, just reach up to the intercessors near you and say, 'thank you, thank you.' I want to say to the intercessors, 'thank you for your faithfulness even when you were unknown; even when we didn't know you were there. Thank you, thank you from the depths of my heart. Thank you!'"

The Need of Reconciliation

As we move into a new millennium sadly much of the church is in disarray. Despite Paul's 2000-year-old admonition against division in the church (see 1 Cor. 12:22-25), anyone can plainly see that the body of Christ is severely splintered. Among the divisions are

⋄ Denominationalism
⋄ Racial tensions
⋄ The gender gap

⬦ The charismatic versus non-charismatic issues
⬦ Minister and laity distinctions

Although the 1990s saw some encouraging movement with issues of reconciliation in the church, the lost world might rightly ask, "Why are these Christians trying to reconcile me to God when they are not even reconciled to each other?" It is an excellent question, and one that deserves an answer. After all, reconciliation implies relationship!

But there is something else. Along with the need for reconciliation, we must offer the Lord new wineskins. God wants to pour out the new wine of revival upon his church. And he has saved the best wine until last. It is a purifying wine, a healing wine, and an empowering wine. New wine however, requires new wineskins. (See Mark 2:22.) As someone has said, "New wineskins are all freshly dead."

Becoming new wineskins requires the personal sacrifice of dying to self. If we really want to live, we must die to ourselves. Becoming new wineskins also requires an abandoning of the old. So the church today is in a state of flux. The only thing we can count on in the future is change. But as long as the church looks like a sieve, fraught with disunity, it will never hold water, much less new wine.

We are on the brink of what may be history's last great revival and a worldwide harvest of souls. God is restoring the very nature of the church (his bride) as he prepares her for earth's final spiritual battle to be followed by the marriage supper of the Lamb.

> The only thing we can count on in the future is change.

However, Jesus said, *"A house divided against itself will fall"* (Luke 11:17). As unity enables, so also disunity disables. For 2000 years a disabled church has tried

⬦ To reach a disabled world
⬦ To fight against the kingdom of darkness
⬦ To complete the Great Commission

Unity enables.
Disunity disables.

As a result of our divisions, we have accomplished surprisingly little. After 2000 years of opportunity, much of the world is yet to know God and the eternal salvation that could be theirs through his Son Jesus Christ. Two thousand more years of the same from the church will produce the same pitiful results! That is precisely why we need to pray for *watchmen* (intercessors) to "stand in the gap" and for *gatekeepers* (pastors), who will move into position to work effectively with them.

Watchmen - The Intercessors
(Isaiah 62:6)

Watchmen (intercessors) are those in the body of Christ who are

- ◇ Primarily committed to the ministry of prayer
- ◇ Tend to be full of faith
- ◇ Are frontline soldiers in the ancient spiritual war between God and Satan
- ◇ Are gifted to see the unseen and discern the works of darkness
- ◇ Passionately pursue God's presence and power

Gatekeepers - Pastors
(1 Chronicles 9)

Gatekeepers (pastors) are those in the body of Christ who are

- ◇ Called and committed to love, to lead and to feed the flock of God
- ◇ Called to administrate the work of the church

- ◇ Carry a natural instinct to protect the body of Christ
- ◇ Leaders who impact the spiritual atmosphere of a city

Since prayer
- ◇ Is foundational to every part of ministry
- ◇ Puts the power of God into the work of God
- ◇ Enforces Christ's victory over his enemies, then the linkage between the ministry of pastor and intercessor is vital to the church's successful completion of its mission

The removal of estrangement between watchmen (intercessors) and gatekeepers (pastors), which we are addressing in this book, is critical to the future success of the church. The relationship of respect, effective communication and meaningful partnership between our pastors and our pray-ers must be restored if the church is to regain her spiritual integrity, to glorify Christ and to demolish the gates of hell.

In nation after nation, city after city, church after church, we have discovered a breakdown between these two important roles. There are many wonderful pastors who love God and their churches. Skillful and effective men of God who confess to us that they simply do not understand the ministry of intercession and therefore have no understanding of their intercessors.

At the conclusion of one of our seminars in California an elderly pastor said to me (Alice), "I've been a pastor for 38 years. Before today, I never knew there were people in my church who love to pray."

Our friends, Ace and Joy Clarke, co-pastors of the Joshua Center in Hamilton, Ontario, Canada have a powerful intercessory prayer ministry. Ace candidly admits, "In the past, I for one have stood *against* intercessors simply because our city has been filled with a plethora of off-based, error-filled teaching. In some cases a calculated attempt was made to lift the intercessor to a higher level of authority than the pastor. Some of our churches suffered under this error and have paid a price for it."

However, there are many intercessors who love God and spend much time in his presence crying out for the needs around them. But they have little understanding of the role of their pastor, the nature of spiritual authority, or any idea how to partner with church leadership. The alienation between them appears to be based on a combination of things including differences in

- ⋄ Spiritual perspectives (how they see and interpret spiritual things)
- ⋄ Spiritual giftedness (how God has equipped them individually to deal with spiritual issues)
- ⋄ Spiritual assignment (the ministries or purposes to which God has called them)

Although not always the case, it is true in the United States today that most pastors are male, and possess organizational skills and gifts, while most intercessors are female, possessing intuitive skills and gifts.

Another reason for this breach is "failed trust." Pastors have knowingly or unknowingly offended intercessors, and intercessors have likewise disappointed their pastors. In some cases this is more than a failure to partner in ministry. It is a matter of jealousy, suspicion, control and a critical spirit.

The ministries of *both* pastors and intercessors are crucial to the health of the church. After all, it was Jesus who said his church was to be a "house of prayer." But tolerance and coexistence between watchmen and gatekeepers is not enough. True reconciliation is a matter of relationship: a relationship of love, respect and collaboration.

My (Eddie) mother was a great cook. She specialized in Southern-style biscuits—specifically, sweet potato biscuits with bacon bits. Excuse me I'm drooling. Now I don't know much, but *I do know biscuits!* You can point to a pile of flour, a cup of milk, an egg, some salt and baking powder and call it biscuits, if you like. The ingredients are all there. But until they are placed in proper relationship with each other and have been through the fire together, *they are not biscuits!* So it is with us!

The Nature of Reconciliation

Jesus prayed that we, his church, would be brought to complete unity (see John 17:23).

◇ It's Not Uniformity

Unity is not uniformity or "sameness." We don't have to believe the same or be the same to walk in Christian unity. We are encouraged to *"Make every effort to keep the unity of the Spirit through the bond of peace"* (Ephesians 4:3). Maintaining unity requires effort because those who dwell together in biblical unity still retain their diversity.

◇ It's More Than Union

Complete unity is more than union. Tie the tails of two alley cats together and toss them across a clothes line, and you have union. But you don't have unity!

In our pastoral experience, we learned that pastors and intercessors are examples to the flock of God. These two groups of admired and respected spiritual people, are uniquely positioned in the church to demonstrate biblical unity and exemplify the extremes to which one should go to maintain this precious commodity at all costs.

Biblical unity is centered on the person, the atoning death and the resurrection of the Lord Jesus Christ, not on our peripheral opinions, personal preferences, gender-biases, or spiritual gifts and callings.

Bound together by love, in the bond of peace, we will graciously agree to disagree about lesser issues when we must. We learn to disagree without being disagreeable and to ask ourselves, "Is this a conviction for which I am willing to die?" Jesus was specific as to both the type and the degree of unity he desires to see in us. What does this unity look like?

1. The unity we are to experience is a *relational unity*. Jesus prayed, *"that all of them may be one, Father, just as you are in me and I am in you"* (John 17:21a).

Jesus and the Father are one, though distinctly different. We are also to be one, even with our *diversity*. Relational unity will allow for individual differences. If I (Eddie), as a pastor refuse to accept my intercessors' uniqueness, then I am rejecting part of who they are.

If I (Alice), as an intercessor refuse my pastor's role in my life, then I am rejecting the ordained authority God has placed in him.

2. We are called to live in *functional unity*. His prayer continues, *"May they also be in us so that the world may believe that you have sent me."*

There is a purpose for this unity. Unlike the ecumenical movement of the seventies when unity *was* our goal, today we have a higher goal than acceptance, tolerance and fellowship. Unity is only a means to an end. Jesus told us what effect a purified and unified church will have on a sin-soaked society. The lost will believe that God has sent him. They will be convinced by our unity and not by our arguments.

Our unity is a picture worth a thousand words. (See John 17 21b.) The plan hasn't changed. There is a function to perform, and a task to complete called the Great Commission (see Matthew 28:19-20).

3. Most importantly, we are called to live in *organic unity*. Simply put, we are not separate; we are grafted into the same Vine.

We are sustained by the same Life Force, if you know Christ. The spiritual Life that flows in us is the same Life that flows in you.

Accomplishing unity is not our job. Christ did that 2000 years ago on Calvary. We are witnesses (see Acts 1:8) who simply *demonstrate* what he has done before men and before demonic deities. (See Ephesians 3:10.)

It is time for us to abandon our declarations of spiritual *independence,* and declare once and for all our spiritual *interdependence.* (See 1 Corinthians 12:12-27.)

The Ministry of Reconciliation

God has given the ministry of reconciliation to each person who knows him. This includes the ministry of evangelism, as we help those without Christ become reconciled to God.

Effective evangelism is dependent upon biblical unity in the church!

But the ministry of reconciliation is first a ministry of unity within the church. As we build bridges over those things that separate us, we bring soundness to the body of Christ so the world may believe in him. Effective evangelism is dependent upon biblical unity in the church. (See Matthew 5:9; John 17:21; 1 Corinthians 12:22-26; 2 Corinthians 5:18.)

> *"All this is from God, who reconciled us to himself through Christ and gave us the ministry of reconciliation: that God was reconciling the world to himself in Christ, not counting men's sins against them. And he has committed to us the message of reconciliation"* (2 Corinthians 5:18-19).

God always puts the responsibility of initiating reconciliation directly upon the shoulders of the one who would draw closer to him.

Reconciliation is never accidental. It's always intentional. It doesn't "just happen." It is a priestly ministry to perform. The reconciler in a relationship, as Jesus was when he reconciled us to God, will always be required to pay the price of humility and at times, even humiliation. Reconciliation requires an initiator and a responder. But God always puts the responsibility of initiating reconciliation directly on the shoulders of the one who would draw closer to him. *"Therefore, if you are offering your gift at the altar and there remember that your brother has something against you, leave your gift there in front of the altar. First go and be reconciled to your brother; then come and offer your gift"* (Matthew 5:23-24). In this passage we see that the Lord will not accept our offering, no matter what it is, if we have not sought to resolve issues with others!

Reconciliation is never easy. In fact, in some cases it requires an abundant measure of God's grace. In his book, *A Gentle Thunder*, author Max Lucado says it well.

Double-tongued promise-breakers.
Fair-weather friends. What they said and what they did are two different things. Oh, maybe they didn't leave you alone at the cross, but maybe they left you alone with the bills…
        or your question
                or your illness.
Or maybe you were just left at the altar,
        or in the cold,
                holding the bag.

Vows forgotten. Contract abandoned.
Logic says: "Put up your fists."
Jesus says: "Fill up the basin."
Logic says: "Bloody his nose."
Jesus says: "Wash his feet."
Logic says: "She doesn't deserve it."
Jesus says: "You're right, but you don't either."

I don't understand how God can be so kind to us, but he is. He kneels before us, takes our feet in his hands, and washes them. Please understand that in washing the disciples' feet, Jesus is washing ours. You and I are in this story. We are at the table. That's us being cleansed, not from our dirt, but from our sins. And the cleansing is not just a gesture; it is a necessity. [1]

The Minister of Reconciliation

Whether you are a pastor or an intercessor, you have been called to the ministry of reconciliation. We encourage you to let God examine your heart and your relationships. Let's pause and take a personal inventory.

Pastor, stop now and ask yourself:
- ◇ Have I exhibited spiritual pride?
- ◇ Have I been (even subtly) controlling? Have I pushed my agenda and methodology on my congregation generally, and my intercessors specifically?
  (Intercessors are not hired guns used to twist God's arm to endorse some man's agenda, but some pas-

tors seem to have that subconscious expectation.)

◇ When "challenged" by my intercessors, do I take offense and ignore them. Do I capitulate to those who are more traditional and are primarily seeking their comfort zone?

◇ Do I know who my people of prayer are?

◇ Have I honestly tried to teach and train the intercessors to use the gifts God has given them? Have I equipped myself with a knowledge and practice of prayer so to be able to teach—by "rule" and example?

◇ Do I honor them? If so, do they know it? Have I acknowledged the place God has given them in our church? Or are they generally ignored instead?

◇ Have I wounded or ridiculed an intercessor?

◇ Am I open to the intercessors and the ministry that God has given them? Are they ministering freely and fruitfully in my church?

◇ Do I "intercede" for my people of prayer?

◇ Am I mindful of and committed to providing spiritual covering for my intercessors--for them personally as well as their ministry?

Intercessor, take a moment and ask yourself:

◇ Have I exhibited spiritual pride? Does the pastor see me as unteachable or unreachable?

◇ Have I been (even subtly) controlling? Have I pushed my revelations and prophecies on my pastor?

◇ Am I committed to submit and pray for my pastors until God releases me, even if I feel they are wrong?

◇ Have I been prone to flamboyant activities that have no real value, and which were not inspired nor instructed by God, for the sake of being seen or heard?

◇ Have I gone around my pastor with my revelations or talked against (gossip) my pastor?

◇ Have I gotten out of timing regarding the things I

felt God was telling me?

◇ Have I been judgmental of my spiritual leaders? Am I wounded and unwilling to forgive those in authority over me?

◇ Do I know my pastor's vision and am I committed to help him achieve it?

◇ Have I lifted my pastor's hands as Aaron and Hur did Moses'?

If you are guilty of any of these issues, stop right now and ask the Lord to forgive you. Then take the proper steps to correct the problems. The pastors and intercessors God will use mightily in the future will be those who display...

1. Teamwork and Unity

We happily report that the day of the ministry "superstar," the "one-man band" is past. We remember a street banner displayed in a small West Virginia town promoting a tent revival. It encouraged everyone to come to the big tent and hear Evangelist So-and-so who, according to the banner, had "all the gifts of the Spirit operating in his life." Anyone with all the gifts operating in his life is not *a member* of the church . . . *he is the church!*

The Apostle Paul wrote, *"For as the body is one, and hath many members, and all the members of that one body, being many, are one body: so also is Christ"* (1 Corinthians 12:12). True spiritual ministry is larger than any single person. It is accomplished by the application of various personalities and spiritual gifts. After all, it is *together* that we are the body of Christ.

Paul wrote, *"In him the whole building is joined together and rises to become a holy temple in the Lord. And in him you too are being built together to become a dwelling in which God lives by his Spirit"* (Ephesians 2:21-22).

2. Servanthood and humility

"A person called on his minister to tell him he did not enjoy his preaching as much as he once did. 'Well, my brother,' said the minister, 'before you tell me what you have to find fault with in me, let us pray together. Will you kneel down and pray for me?'

They knelt down and prayed, and when they arose, the minister said: 'Now, my brother, sit down and tell me what fault you have to find.'

The man said, 'I'm ashamed of myself. I have no fault to find at all.' The man continued, 'Why, sir, since you have asked me to pray for you I cannot find fault with you; I believe now, the fault is in myself. I never prayed for you before, but now I will.'" [2]

The pastor showed humility by refusing to defend himself. His accuser was drawn to servanthood by his pastor's humility. This is the attitude on which godly relationships are developed. (See Isaiah 53:7.)

3. Dependence upon the Holy Spirit

If you would become a minister of reconciliation you must strive to maintain your own spiritual life and personal intimacy with God in order to know his will. You must renounce your personal "declaration of *independence*" in order to function *interdependently* with the body of Christ to do the work of the ministry. *Together* we must totally *depend* upon the Holy Spirit's guidance and his power for the results.

4. Integrity and accountability

As we enter a new millennium, nothing better describes the qualifications of a ministry leader, be it a pastor or an intercessor, than does an article from Belfast, Ireland's Weekly Telegram.

Twenty-first Century leaders must have . . .
⋄ "The strength of an ox;
⋄ The tenacity of a bulldog;
⋄ The daring of a lion;
⋄ The patience of a donkey;
⋄ The industry of a beaver;
⋄ The versatility of a chameleon;
⋄ The vision of an eagle;
⋄ The meekness of a lamb;
⋄ The hide of a rhinoceros;
⋄ The disposition of an angel;
⋄ The resignation of an incurable;
⋄ The loyalty of an apostle;
⋄ The heroism of a martyr;
⋄ The faithfulness of a prophet;
⋄ The tenderness of a shepherd;
⋄ The fervency of an evangelist;
And, the devotion of a mother."[2]

While being interviewed on a local cable television channel recently I (Eddie) was explaining about intercessors and their unique ministry in the church. The interviewer, a local pastor said with a critical tone, "Yeah, those intercessors are a weird group, aren't they?"

His comment hit me wrong and I said, "Pastor, you're like some others I know. You want the advantages of having intercessors in your church. But you want all your intercessors delivered to you 'fully grown' so you don't have the responsibility to pastor them. Thank God there were spiritual people around to mentor and guide you as a young pastor." (I think the pastor got the idea.)

Years ago we conducted meetings in several churches near a major theological seminary. Those precious people never had a pastor who was more than 30 years of age. Because of their proximity to the school, they always had "student pastors." Through the years, the patient people in those churches had tolerated and cleaned up the messes of dozens of young pastors-in-training.

Pastor, your intercessors have no seminary. They have few mentors and models. You will have to provide for their training, and clean up their messes from time to time.

The ministry of intercession is as old as mankind. From Exodus 32 when Moses pled before the Lord on behalf of the Children of Israel, to Luke 2:37 when Anna *"departed not from the temple, but served God with fastings and prayers night and day,"* intercessors have faithfully stood in the gap. There has always been a remnant in the church that has faithfully accepted God's intercessory assignments.

Yet the current public movement of intercession in the United States is little more than 10 years old. Until the 1990s there was very little written or taught about prayer. Many intercessors had to learn from trial and error. They had few mentors, many questions and spent lots of lonely hours feeling something strange was going on in their hearts. They knew their calling was different, but they didn't understand. Since most pastors are not intercessors, few even knew how to help them. Pastor, we trust that books like this will assist you as you lead these vitally necessary people in your church.

Pastor, you are a spiritual gatekeeper in your home, your church and your city. You are one of the elders at the spiritual gates of your city. Ask God to enlarge your vision.

Limited vision will produce limited results!

Begin to see the spiritual territory for which you are responsible.

Intercessor, you are a spiritual watchman of your church, your city and possibly the nation. Think big! Too many of us have "tunnel vision." Limited vision will produce limited results!

As Old Testament watchmen and gatekeepers worked together for the protection of the city, we are seeing God reestablish this strategic partnership of pastors and intercessors for ministry in the days ahead.

We have looked at the division, the need for reconciliation and the nature of the relationship God is restoring, especially between intercessors and pastors. But how will this partnership of watchmen and gatekeepers affect our churches and cities? In Scripture God uses many metaphors to describe his church. He calls us . . .

- ◇ a temple
- ◇ a family
- ◇ a body
- ◇ a bride

In the next chapter we will offer another metaphor for the church...a *protective spiritual wall* for our cities. As we look at the walls, the gates and the watchtowers, we will get a better understanding of the roles of the watchmen and gatekeepers.

CHAPTER TWO

The City Walls

To understand the important relationship between the watch-men and the gatekeepers, let's travel back in our imaginations to Old Testament times and look at the physical make-up of the ancient walled cities.

You'll remember that when Joshua and the Children of Israel entered the Promised Land, they discovered cities that were surrounded with strongly fortified protective stone walls. Archeologists tell us that although those walls were rarely load-bearing, they were often very high. They were designed to keep out enemy forces. In Deuteronomy 1:28 Moses de-scribed cities as having *"walls to the sky."*

The walls were not only high; they were wide and built to last. We are told that the walls of Nineveh were so wide that three chariots abreast could be driven atop them. Babylon's walls were said to be so wide that six chariots could be driven side by side atop them. These city walls were built of layers of stones placed in courses, one on top of the other.

During a prayer journey to Turkey my (Alice) team and I were taken to the excavated walls of cities that were built in the 5th century BC. Although the cities are no longer occu-pied, the foundations and walls remain intact. They have with-stood the ravages of time, weather and even severe earth-quakes. When the foundation is solid, the walls will withstand the greatest of shakings. There is a spiritual analogy to con-sider.

The Church, a Protective Wall for the City

Like those ancient city walls, Peter describes believers in similar terms. He says that we are "living stones" that God has spiritually built together, with Christ being our "Chief Cornerstone." In a sense, God has built us together to provide salvation and spiritual security for the inhabitants of our cities. (See 1 Samuel 25:16; Isaiah 26:1, 60:18; 1 Peter 2:5.)

Remember that the city of Sodom could have been spared had there been enough righteous people living there. We, the church, are those who have been made righteous by the blood of Christ. Because of this, we are responsible to provide spiritual security for our cities by our righteous living. (See Genesis 18:16-33; 2 Corinthians 5:17, 21.)

Untempered Mortar

Mortar was of particular importance to the ancient walls. They were sometimes weakened by the use of "untempered mortar." Carefully read these verses.

> "Because, even because they have seduced my people, saying, Peace; and there was no peace; and one built up a wall, and, lo, others daubed it with untempered mortar: Say unto them which daub it with untempered mortar, that it shall fall . . .. So will I break down the wall that ye have daubed with untempered mortar, and bring it down to the ground, so that the foundation thereof shall be discovered . . . Thus will I accomplish my wrath upon the wall, and upon them that have daubed it with untempered mortar, and will say unto you, The wall is no more, neither they that daubed it" (Ezekiel 13:10-15 KJV).

No wall is stronger than the mortar that holds each stone in place. But what is meant by "untempered mortar?" Untempered mortar is untested mortar. Untempered mortar may be mortar that has been watered down or in some other way compromised in its formation.

Ezekiel reports that walls built with untempered mortar *will* fall. In fact, verse 14 says that God *himself* will break them down. "Would any of us want to spend our lives building walls that God has promised to break down?" And yet tragically many of us have, and some of us are building them right now.

One of the weaknesses in the body of Christ today is the untempered mortar that binds us together. Now, we are not necessarily addressing the untempered mortar of which Ezekiel spoke. We are referring to an untempered mortar many Christians are using to build relationships today…which is *misplaced trust*.

Christians in almost every congregation and city are attempting to build relationships with the untempered mortar of *trust*. They are busy trying to find people they deem trustworthy.

At the same time, people are trying to prove to others that they (themselves) can be trusted. As one pastor in the Northwest said, "We pastors who are meeting together monthly for prayer are learning to *trust one another.*"

A pastor called one day with great news. He is a precious man who had suffered a run of bad church experiences. "I've been called to a new church. We are really blessed to be here. This church has four deacons and three of them are solidly on our side," he said excitedly.

"Write down their names," I (Eddie) replied.

"Write down their names! Why?" He asked.

"Because, they will be the very ones who will run you off!" I explained. And in a short time they did.

Why did I say that? Because it was clear that he was trusting in his new deacons for job security. And God will not

> Whether we trust ourselves, or place our trust in others, trusting man will never securely bind us together. It will always result in disappointment.

allow us to trust *anyone* but him.

Trusting others is untempered mortar. Whether we place our trust in ourselves, or in someone else, trusting people will never securely bind us together. It will always result in disappointment.

As Ezekiel points out, God himself will tear down walls built with untempered mortar. Why would he tear down our trust-based relationships? It's quite simple really. The Lord is jealous of our trust. We are to *trust* in the Lord with all of our heart, and to *love* each other. Listen to these striking verses:

⋄ *"It is better to take refuge in the Lord than to trust in princes"* (Psalm 118:9).
⋄ *"Trust in the Lord with all your heart..."* (Proverbs 3:5).

On the other hand, Jesus taught:

⋄ *"'Love the Lord your God with all your heart and with all your soul and with all your mind.' This is the first and greatest commandment. And the second is like it: 'Love your neighbor as yourself.' All the Law and the prophets hang on these two commandments"* (Matthew 22:37-39).

Paul wrote, *"And over all these virtues put on love, which binds them all together in perfect unity"* (Colossians 3:14). *Love* is the mortar that should bind us together. The church needs a transfusion of God's love. Not just to know that God loves us, but to commit to deeply loving each other.

How do we know that God loves us? Because John 3:16 declares that he laid down his life for us. How then does he know that we love him? We prove our love for God by our willingness to lay down our lives for each other! (See 1 John 3:16.)

We've all had friends who were ready to lay down *our lives* for their issue or cause. But rare is the friend who will lay down his or her life for us.

> Relationship is the heart of the Gospel. Love is the heart of relationship.

Relationship is the heart of the Gospel. The first is our relationship with the Father. The second is our relationships with each other. And love is the heart of these relationships. As a wall is built one stone at a time, relationships are built one at a time. Meaningful relationships are woven together with the fibers of selflessness and servanthood.

Some years ago I (Eddie) was invited to attend a meeting for minority pastors that a major international ministry leader had called in Dallas, Texas. With great enthusiasm this gracious leader encouraged, then implored these pastors to mobilize their men to attend his stadium event.

In his inimitably passionate and dramatic manner he ended his appeal tearfully on his knees before this group of around 30 pastors.

He had poured out his soul before them. And it seemed like an eternity before one of the older Afro-American pastors finally stood to respond.

"Sir," he explained, "I almost didn't come to this meeting today. I assumed it would be just another meeting set up by some guys like yourself to push your agenda on us. People like you always form your committees, plan your things and then at the last minute you ask us to participate. But we've learned we can't trust you. If you expect to get us involved, you've got a big job ahead of you." With that he sat down leaving the room uncomfortably charged with anxiety.

My host leaned over and asked me quietly, "Eddie, would you like to respond to the Bishop's charge?" I nodded yes. He said, "Go ahead."

I walked over to where the Bishop was seated. "Sir, with respect I must correct something you've just said. You are quite right that people like our host and me have offended and taken advantage of people like you. But Bishop, God knows that we are mere men, and that we cannot ultimately be trusted. We are going to eventually disappoint anyone who puts their trust in us.

In fact Bishop, I've never yet met a man or woman, black or white that I could trust. Eventually they all let me down in some form or fashion. I even let myself down from time to time. Perhaps that's why God never tells us to put our trust in each other.

Rather, he tells us that we are to trust in him alone and to love each other, as we love ourselves. Sir, you are the one with a big job ahead of you. You are challenged with loving brothers and sisters in Christ who you cannot trust?'" As I returned to my seat, the tension eased as the Bishop thoughtfully nodded having received my words with grace.

Immediate versus Ultimate Trust

We saw a man wearing a tee shirt at the mall that read, "Never trust anybody." It's a little hard to get along in this world without trusting anybody.

However, we must learn the difference between *immediate trust* and *ultimate trust*. For an example, we place our *immediate trust* in the airline pilot to fly us safely from point A to point B, however our *ultimate trust* is in the Lord.

We *immediately trust* the youth pastor and sponsors to care for our children at youth camp, but our *ultimate trust* is in the Lord.

We *immediately trust* our spouse to be faithful to our marriage covenant, but our *ultimate trust* is in the Lord. Ultimately, we must trust the Lord in all things.

Sadly, many suffer today because they have continually placed their trust in man and had it shattered in the process. As one lady told us, "Every man I've ever trusted has let me down."

Here was someone who had been looking all her life for a man she could trust. As soon as she found one, he proved to be untrustworthy. She had moved from heartbreak to heartbreak until she no longer was willing to enter into a meaningful relationship with any man.

She had never seen that the men were not the problem. The problem was that she was attempting to build with untempered mortar. Her whole system was flawed. She was trying in vain to find a man she could trust. She had always been seen as the victim, when in fact, the men in her past may have been victimized by her "need" to trust someone. She had to be redirected to look for a man she would love, not one she could trust.

When we were in the pastorate I (Eddie) half-jokingly told our church members, "Go ahead and forgive me now, I promise, I will let you down. And by the way, I have already forgiven you. I will never hold a grudge against you. Nor will I ever harbor unforgiveness or resentment toward you. I will love you regardless of what you do."

Although I seek to live a trustworthy life, Christ and his Lordship in me is my only claim to trustworthiness. As pastors we must sow unconditional love into our intercessors if we expect to receive unconditional love from them.

If you are having trouble in one of your relationships today, check it out. You may discover that you are suffering because you have trusted that person to perform according to your standards, rather than loving them

> Love means stepping out on a limb, which you know may well be cut off.

unconditionally. It's not an easy thing to love unconditionally. To navigate the emotions, summon the courage and surrender it all to God will require the fullness of the Holy Spirit in your life.

Love means stepping out on a limb, which you know may well be cut off. It means becoming vulnerable to disappointment, hurt and grief. Love is never free. It always carries a price tag. Jesus loved us enough to suffer. That is true love.

It is time for Christians to begin to love each other as Christ loves.

Pastor, we realize how hard it is to reestablish relationships after so many times of feeling betrayed and abandoned. For this reason many pastors and Christian leaders have dropped out of the ministry altogether. But when your trust is in the Lord, although grief and disappointment will follow the loss of a cherished friendship, there won't be total devastation. Peter writes, *"Above all, love each other deeply, because love covers over a multitude of sins"* (1 Peter 4:8).

Intercessor, we realize how hard it is to risk with a leader who may have accused you of witchcraft praying or worse, completely ignored you. But it is easier to give what you think the Lord has shown you to leaders and then fully release it, when your trust is in the Lord Jesus. The final outcome is not your responsibility. The act of obedience is.

Failed Trust is Love's Test

However, even love is untempered (untested) until it has gone through the fiery trial of relational difficulty. The disappointment of failed trust puts love to the test. The real question is, "Can I love someone who I cannot trust?" God does. He loves us.

Our ability to trust God and love people, even those we cannot trust, is one measure of our maturity. God will never compete with others for our trust. Again, our God is a jealous God! (See Zechariah 1:14.) He wants to see our love mature, so he will see to it that our "trust in man" fails, whether we are trusting in ourselves or in someone else.

Accepting our Judas'

Do you have a Judas in your life? Have you had a Judas? Almost all of us have been betrayed at one time or another by someone we trusted. Jesus had his and we can rest assured that we will have ours (see Hebrews 2:18).

Jesus was tempted as we are. He suffered and we should expect to suffer with him. *"If we suffer, we shall also reign with him"* (2 Timothy 2:12). Why are we betrayed from time to time?

1. We suffer betrayal in order *to prove that our faith is genuine.* What is faith? Faith is not trusting in people, who we can see. Faith is "the evidence of things not seen"…God! Faith is trust in God alone. *"In this you greatly rejoice, though now for a little while you may have had to suffer grief in all kinds of trials. These have come so that your faith—of greater worth than gold, which perishes even though refined by fire—may be proved genuine and may result in praise, glory and honor when Christ Jesus is revealed"* (1 Peter 1:6-7). Peter convinces us that fiery trials refine and purify our faith.

2. Our suffering is *to result in praise, glory and honor to God.* It is after all, the broken vessel that releases the precious perfume. If we have no trials, then we have no triumphs. The trials of life provide us with the opportunity to be overcomers.

3. We are tested in order that we might *develop perseverance and spiritual maturity.* *"Consider it pure joy, my brothers, whenever you face trials of many kinds, because you know that the testing of your faith develops perseverance. Perseverance must finish its work so that you may become mature and complete, not lacking anything"* (James 1:2-4).

So how should we respond when we are betrayed? Peter and James tell us to rejoice. In order to do this we must have the long view and not the short view of life. Let's consider how Jesus dealt with his Judas.

◇ When Jesus was betrayed his *first concern was for the purposes of God*. He took no thought of himself. In one sense, Jesus had effectively died in the Garden of Gethsemane when he surrendered his will to the will of the Father.

> Can a person who has betrayed me and neither sought nor been willing to accept reconciliation, continue to be my friend?

His death to self, through total commitment to the purposes of the Father, no doubt lessened the pain of his betrayal. And so will ours. Dying to self is a powerful weapon against Satan (see Revelation 12:11).

◇ Jesus' second concern was for his *betrayer, Judas*. Even as Judas betrayed him, amazingly Jesus called him his friend (see Matthew 26:50). Even when we betray Jesus, he still calls us his friends.

In some cases of wounded or broken relationships reconciliation is possible. In other cases, as it was with Jesus and Judas, reconciliation isn't possible. But God's grace to cope is still available to prevent our harboring unforgiveness, resentment and bitterness.

The test: Can a person who has betrayed me and neither sought nor been willing to accept reconciliation, continue to be my friend? The answer should be yes.

◇ Jesus' third concern was for *the High Priest's servant*. At a time when he could have been bitter with his betrayer and angry at the prospects of his pending brutal death, Jesus compassionately stopped and restored the ear that an enraged Simon Peter had severed with a sword. (Luke 22:50-51; John 18:10) In contrast, we have seen countless ministers who after being betrayed by those they loved, drop completely out of the ministry because of their pain.

It may be extremely difficult, but even while experiencing betrayal by someone we love, we can exercise genuine forgiveness and compassion. This is only possible when we are being filled with the Holy Spirit.

How could Jesus act with such selflessness? He was able to do so because he wasn't trusting Judas. Jesus' trust was in his Father. In death, many of his closest friends abandoned him. Yet he even loved his executioners while trusting God alone.

Right now, pause and thank God for your Judas. You may be thinking, "Are you crazy?" The truth is this. Like Jesus, each of us needs a Judas to help us get to our cross--the cross on which we die to ourself. (See Matthew 16:24; Romans 6:11; Galatians 2:20.) For as we die to self, then the resurrected Christ can reign in us. When Christ reigns in us, our relationships with others will be built with the tempered mortar of love.

Is it Live or is it Memorex?

If you are old enough you might recall the cassette tape commercial that posed the question, "Is it live, or is it Memorex (taped)?" Sometimes it is difficult to judge whether we have been building with the *true mortar* of love or the *untempered mortar* of trust. We would like to suggest the following test.

When a relationship is tested, does it produce anger or grief in your heart? Hey, let's be real…at first you may feel anger. However, you cannot stay angry with one you truly love. You can only ultimately experience grief. Grief, after all, is a love word.

How do you know whether your damaged relationship is based on trust or love? Here is the test: Betrayed *trust* produces anger. Betrayed *love* produces grief. Unmanaged anger leads to resentment and resentment leads to bitterness. Grief, on the other hand, opens the way to engage in genuine intercessory prayer for the situation.

Perhaps you are a pastor who has placed your trust in a person. A trusted intercessor let you down, or betrayed your confidence. Begin to recognize that the problem was not so much their lack of trustworthiness as it was your decision to trust rather than to love them. For if you truly love your people of prayer you will offer them room to fail, and a fresh supply of forgiveness when they need it.

Or you may be an intercessor who has been betrayed or unfairly rebuked by a pastor. Pastors are people too. Whether you were intentionally or unintentionally wounded, the pain of the offense is just the same. Even now you can choose to express Christ's love and forgiveness.

In Ezekiel 13:10-13 we learned that the untempered mortar of trust will not endure the tests that our relationships are sure to face. Love will. Ezekiel 13:5 says, *"You have not gone up to the breaks in the wall to repair it…so that it will stand firm in the battle on the day of the Lord."* It is time for us to repair and rebuild the walls of our relationships with love, grace and understanding in which we consider each other better than ourselves (see Philippians 2:3). Our challenge is to close the breaks in the wall with forgiveness. Why? Ezekiel says it is so we can stand firm in the battle on the day of the Lord.

Strong secure spiritual walls, built with the mortar of God's love and forgiveness, are being built in cities around the world. Pastors are coming together across denominational, cultural and racial lines to forge partnerships with Christ's love in order to complete the Great Commission and to extend the Kingdom of God in their cities.

Pastors and intercessors are doing the same. These walls of love will indeed pass the tests as we choose to stand in the gap for each other. In the next chapter we'll consider the ancient city gates and the purpose God intends for the gatekeepers.

CHAPTER THREE

The Ancient Gates

The gates of the ancient cities were strategically placed along the walls to allow entrance into and exit out of the city. These gates were significant structures constructed of iron, brass and wood. They were fortified with beams, doors, locks and bars. The word "massive" best describes them.

A single gate could be composed of from four to six chambers or rooms. The gate complex at the city of Dan, for example, measured 58 by 97 feet. That's more than 32 yards wide.

These gates seemed strong enough. However, they were isolated from each another. Therefore, the gates were actually the weakest points in the cities' walls and were usually the first places to be attacked.

The gates of the fortified city of Gaza also appeared strong. Yet one muscleman, Samson, was able to carry one of those city gates on his shoulders to the top of a hill. (See Judges 16:3.)

For a moment, let's imagine that these gates represent the individual local churches (or congregations) in your city. If your city is like most American cities, you will find that our past "turfism" and independent spirit has kept many of our churches isolated. Isolationism has left them powerless; so powerless that they have little or no impact on the daily lives and struggles of the cities' inhabitants.

Many years ago we were attempting to plant a church in a fast-growing part of northwest Houston. Another church (of our own denomination) heard that we were looking to buy property approximately one-half mile from their campus. Immediately, they began circulating a petition to the pastors of other churches in our denomination in an effort to prevent us from buying property there.

One pastor, angry about the petition said, "Why I wouldn't mind if another church was built across the street from ours. As far as that goes, they could even utilize what's left of our parking lot on Sundays!" Obviously, that pastor understood Kingdom concepts! Unfortunately, the other pastor hadn't!

The Purposes of the Gates

The gates of the ancient walls served many purposes. They were meeting places for various activities.

◇ *Judges sat at the gates. So court was frequently held there.* As sin was judged at the ancient city gates, it's time for sin to be judged in our churches.

Local pastors need to unite across denominational and ethnic lines to confront city government leaders when necessary, concerning sin in our cities. It is time for the church's voice to be heard. Christians are to be "salt and light" (see Matthew 5:13-14). We are to set the moral standard for society, not cower from it. (See Deuteronomy 16:18, 17:8, 21:19; 2 Samuel 15:2; Proverbs 22:22-23.)

◇ *Prophets frequently delivered their messages at the gates.* As proclamations were made at the Old Testament cities' gates, today's pastors and churches must effectively proclaim the life-giving Gospel of Jesus Christ to the people who live in our cities. Millions of neighborhood houses of prayer (or Lighthouses) are being launched today. Through this ministry, Christians pray for the five families on either side of their home and the ten families across the street. The three phases of Lighthouses are: prayer, care and share. On a foundation of prayer, they begin to care for the needs of their neighbors and look for ways to present the Gospel.

One of the most effective ways that Churches are presenting the Gospel today is through the distribution of the

Jesus Video in their neighborhoods. (See Appendix A for contact information on these exciting ministries.) (See Proverbs 1:21, 8:3; Jeremiah 17:19-20, 26:10.)

◊ *Real estate transactions were conducted at the gates.* Land was redeemed there. It was a place of restoration. Extending the Kingdom of God is in one sense, a real estate issue! *"For the earth will be filled with the knowledge of the glory of the LORD, as the waters cover the sea"* (Habakkuk 2:14).

There are 1,489 references to the word *land* and 906 references to the word *earth* in the King James Version of the Bible. Land is important to God. *"The earth is the Lord's and the fullness thereof"* (Psalm 24:1).

The Lord is interested in the people who live on the land. The model of Joshua leading the Israelites into battle was about physical real estate. But now the Lord is asking us to take spiritual land away from the enemy. Land that he has stolen.

Defiled Land

In the Old Testament we read *of defiled land.* For millennia Satan has been staking his claim on planet Earth, marking it with the acts of wicked men. As a "squatter" (one who settles on land without right, title or payment of rent), the devil claims ownership of all the souls therein. God clearly tells us how land becomes defiled.

◊ Adultery defiles the land. *" . . . You have defiled the land with your prostitution and wickedness."* (Jeremiah3:2b). Adultery has defiled the United States of America via movies, television, pop music and pornography, (especially Internet porn). American society, its government and even our churches are polluted by sexual sins that are detestable to God. (See Jeremiah 3:9, 7:30.)

⬥ Shedding innocent blood defiles the land. *"Yea, they sacrificed their sons and their daughters unto devils, and shed innocent blood, even the blood of their sons and of their daughters, whom they sacrificed unto the idols of Canaan: and the land was polluted with blood"* (Psalm 106:37-38). Parts of our nation have been built on the bloody massacre sites of Native Americans and land that was soaked with the blood of innocent men who were lynched without trial.

More recently, the shootings in our public schools, bombings in our workplaces and the dragging death of an innocent man in Jasper, Texas have defiled our land. In Habakkuk 2:12 God says, *"Woe to him who builds a town with bloodshed, who establishes a city by iniquity."* War, rape, murder and abuse have saturated our cities.

Our present defilement is partly due to the millions of unborn Americans who are murdered each year by their own mothers at the hands of abortionists before they take their first breath! (See Jeremiah 7:6-7.)

⬥ Broken covenants and treaties defile the land. *"Then there was a famine in the days of David three years, year after year; and David inquired of the LORD. And the LORD answered, It is for Saul, and for his bloody house, because he slew the Gibeonites"* (2 Samuel 21:1). King Saul had disregarded the peace treaty that Joshua had made with the Gibeonites and had them killed. (See Joshua 9:15.) Once King David obeyed the Lord by offering an atonement to the Gibeonites, 2 Samuel 21:14 says, *"After that, God answered prayer on behalf of the land."*

According to the Grolier Encyclopedia, the United States government is responsible for making and then breaking more than 389 treaties with the Native Americans.[1] There are perhaps more.

⬥ Idolatry defiles the land. *"Thou art become guilty in thy blood that thou hast shed; and hast defiled thyself in thine idols which thou hast made . . ."* (Ezekiel 22:4a KJV). It is a sad day for the church in America. We chide the ancient Israelites for having had their household idols, yet we are no different.

Our idols take the form of careers, cars, money, amusement and the works of our own hands. (See Ezekiel 20:31, 36:18.)

Pastor, it is time for the church to offer up prayers that will affect the foundations of the land. Fervent prayers of repentance and petition that actually cleanse the land from its defilement and enable the people who live on it to respond to the Gospel, cannot be prayed exclusively within the four walls of the church. (See Numbers 16:46-48.)

> Intercessory prayer teams must take to the streets, the alleys, the roads, and the mountaintops to repent the land!

Intercessory prayer teams must take to the streets, alleys, roads, and the mountaintops to repent the land. This issue of redeeming the land is the last great job of the church. As we extend God's Kingdom and declare his glory in the whole earth through intercessory prayerwalks and praise marches, the blessings of God will be restored and Satan's grip on the nations will be broken. As we prayerwalk our nation, repent for our sins and the sins of our fathers as Nehemiah did (see Nehemiah 1:6-7), and in unity and purity proclaim the Gospel of the Kingdom, Satan's gates will fall. The churches' gates will be strong and secure. We have God's guarantee on it. (See Matthew 16:18.) At that point, the world's last great spiritual harvest will occur.

Dutch Sheets, in his book *Intercessory Prayer* writes,

> "Sue Doty shared the following testimony regarding doing spiritual warfare in her city. She stepped forward!
>
> 'I sensed the Lord wanted me, along with a team of intercessors to go on a prayer walk over a specific route, but that some

preparation was necessary. First, I talked with my pastor about this and then went to drive along the route I knew we were to prayerwalk. As I approached a theater (X-rated movie house, video shop and bookstore) the Holy Spirit started to give me specific instructions. He told me to cast out the spirits of pornography and lust, and I did so. He also told me to pray in the Spirit. After a short time I was released from praying, and I continued on the rest of the route before going home.

On that Friday the Lord revealed to me what had actually happened. I turned on the local news to hear that this particular theater had been ordered by the city to close its doors. The day after I had been there to pray, the city conducted a surprise inspection. The theater was cited for several violations and its doors were immediately closed and locked.

What was so remarkable was that the city had already inspected the building a short time before and it had passed inspection. But without warning, and for no apparent reason, it was being inspected again. God had really moved! The theater did meet code violations and was reopened for a short period of time before a judge ordered it to close for one year. Now the property is up for sale.

I had taken the course 'Intercessory Prayer—The Lightning of God' by Dutch Sheets and I knew many charges had been placed on the wall, but this was the *kairos* time and the wall fell under the power of God.' (By 'charges' she is referring to the *dunamis*—dyna-

mite—of the Holy Spirit that I teach about in
the previously mentioned course.)"[2]

The church has accepted the concept of God redeeming people, but it has little understanding of the importance
of God redeeming the land. The Apostle Paul wrote,

> *"And, having made peace through the blood of his
> cross, by him to reconcile <u>all things</u> (not just people)
> unto himself; by him, I say, whether they be things
> in earth, or things in heaven"* (Colossians 1:20).

> *"And I sought for a man among them, that should
> make up the hedge, and* **stand in the gap be-
> fore me for the land,** *that I should not destroy
> it: but I found none"* (Ezekiel 22:30).

The message is clear. The call has been extended. Will
you accept the challenge to stand in the gap for the land? As
author and prayer leader Steve Hawthorne says, "It's time for
us to begin praying the prayers that our grand children will be
glad we prayed!"

The Modern Gates

Some churches, like those massive Old Testament gates, appear strong with their enormous buildings, multiple staffs and
creative programs. These churches can be very impressive. But
looks can be deceiving. The church is a living spiritual organism, not a human organization. A strong declaration for vi-
brant, living churches is powerfully stated in this poem.

"STAND YOUR GROUND, O CHURCH! The enemy is on the rampage again… STAND YOUR GROUND! Let neither fear nor adversity daunt your mission! STAND YOUR GROUND! The cesspools of immorality and ungodliness are overflowing, but STAND YOUR GROUND!

The deceiving friends of lethargy and apathy have never been more present, but STAND YOUR GROUND! The godless cults are moving like a prairie fire to consume the immature. But, O CHURCH, STAND YOUR GROUND! Humanistic ideologies are running rampant to twist and warp the minds of our youth today, but STAND YOUR GROUND, O CHURCH. Satan's onslaught against marriage and the family is setting new records, but STAND YOUR GROUND!

Greed, lust, violence, murder, rape, perversion, drunkenness, pornography, lying, adultery and fraud are all having their day right now, but dear church, STAND YOUR GROUND! Wolves in sheep's clothing have come within your gates and in some places stand within your pulpits. But, O CHURCH, STAND YOUR GROUND!

Much of your membership is at ease in Zion while many others are only playing church…but STAND YOUR GROUND, O CHURCH! The world system stands to oppose you, kings and governments legislate to limit you and most of the populace still ignores you, but STAND YOUR GROUND, DEAR

CHURCH, STAND YOUR GROUND! O church...remember who you are...a kingdom that cannot be shaken, a people to be reckoned with, a force that the gates of hell cannot hold back...an invincible army...an indestructible organism that cannot be obliterated or detoured.

O Dear church soon and very soon anti-Christs will appear to put the finishing touches to your demise, (or so they think), so...STAND YOUR GROUND! Hold high your head. Remember your foundation. Keep ever before you, your ultimate destiny. And when the battle's done, the blood of your last martyr has dried, the noise of war has abated and the dust has settled, You, Dear church, will stand! Scarred? Yes! Bruised? Weary? To be sure! But victorious and triumphant, you will stand, with sword drawn, your crown in place, and the enemy slain! So...here and now...in the midst of the battle, STAND YOUR GROUND, O CHURCH, STAND YOUR GROUND!"[3]

Stand your ground church. Let's not be so enamored with our church activities, agendas and accomplishments (that demonstrate little of the power of God), that we confuse the dust of our human activity with the smoke of his holy presence!

As an individual is strengthened by meaningful, life-giving relationships with others, a congregation is strengthened by meaningful, life-giving relationships between pastors and intercessors. Satan knows that if he can keep pastors and intercessors isolated, suspicious and critical of each other by fostering disunity, he can spiritually breach the congregation's walls. We must not let this happen!

Let's re-cap. The protective spiritual walls of our cities describe the body of Christ. As living stones, we are set one upon the other. Our relationships should be bound with the tempered mortar of love, not trust. Trust-based relationships are destined to disappointment and failure. The spiritual gates of our city, our individual congregations, are to dwell together in unity and stand together against any activity that would defile the land. The gates of hell cannot prevail against the church that has posted intercessory watchmen on the walls and pastoral gatekeeperrs protecting the gates.

Now that we understand the walls and the gates...let's learn the roles of the watchmen and gatekeepers!

CHAPTER FOUR

Watchmen and Gatekeepers

Two watchtowers flanked each of the gates of the ancient cities. For example, one of Jerusalem's walls had 90 watchtowers that were manned by watchmen day and night. These watchtowers were considered so important to the health and protection of people in the city that, if it were ever necessary, the building materials from personal homes would be sacrificed in order to repair and fortify them. (See 2 Kings 9:17; Isaiah 62:6-12.)

Our cities today are being overrun with wickedness and violence. What level of sacrifice are we making to staff our intercessory watchtowers?

◇ Does your church care enough about prayer and its necessity to the spiritual health and well-being of your community that your church has built and is staffing a prayer room?

◇ Have you learned that prayer is more than a Christian discipline, that it is actually a spiritual ministry?

◇ What are you doing about prayerwalking and establishing neighborhood houses of prayer or Lighthouses?

The watchtowers beside each gate housed the watchmen who guarded the city day and night. The watchmen were to sound an alarm if they saw an enemy approaching. (See 2 Samuel 18:26; 2 Kings 9:17; Ezekiel 33:2-3.)

"I have set watchmen upon thy walls, O Jerusalem, (watchmen were the city's early warning devices.) *which shall never hold their peace day nor night: ye that make mention of the LORD, keep not silence"* (Isaiah 62:6 KJV).

Who were the watchmen? In a spiritual sense, Israel's *prophets* saw themselves as watchmen. They were the ones who warned the nation of God's impending judgment if the people did not repent.

However, *soldiers* were the ones who generally served as the watchmen in the cities' watchtowers. Notice the similarity to those God has called into the ministry of intercession. Intercessors are prophetic, frontline soldiers in God's army. (See Matthew 27:65-66.)

The word watchman comes from a Hebrew word *tsaphah* meaning "to lean forward, to peer into the distance, to observe, to behold, to spy, or to wait for." This is a wonderful description of an intercessor.

Those of us who are not necessarily gifted intercessors are not exempt from the responsibility of interceding for our cities. For sometimes, as in the case of Nehemiah's rebuilding of the city, *civilians* also served as watchmen. (See Nehemiah 7:3.)

Jim Goll offers more in his book, *The Lost Art of Intercession*. He writes,

> "The Greek word for 'watch' in these verses is *gregoreuo*, and it means 'to be vigilant, wake, to be watchful.' A watchman on the wall does many things. He carefully watches what is happening and alerts the community when good ambassadors approach the city. The guardsman then will open the gates and lower the bridge so the ambassadors may enter. A watchman also warns the city, far in advance when an enemy approaches. He sounds an alarm to awaken the people because he knows 'to forewarn them is to alert and arm them.' Then they quickly can rally to

> take their stand on the wall against the enemy
> before he wrongfully tries to enter into the
> city."[1]

Intercessor, as one of God's watchmen you likely experience from time to time some of the revelatory gifts like prophecy and discerning spirits. These spiritual gifts come from the more controversial "manifestation gifts" listed in 1 Corinthians 12. For this reason, intercessors can be easily misunderstood.

As an example, you may often see things a year or two or more in advance. *"For the vision is yet for an appointed time; but at the end it will speak, and it will not lie. Though it tarries, wait for it; because it will surely come, it will not tarry"* (Habakkuk 2:3). Like the sons of Issachar, you must also be discerning of the times. *"Men of Issachar, who understood the times and knew what Israel should do..."* (1 Chronicles 12:32).

Occasionally you may receive words from the Lord concerning your church. Some of the words you receive should be shared with your pastors. Most of the words you receive however are for your own personal intercession and are to be shared with no one but God.

As I (Alice) write in my book *Beyond the Veil*, "I believe intercessors who have developed a close relationship with Jesus Christ have learned to be trustworthy with the information God shares with them. They have learned to hold 80 percent of what they receive from the Lord and reveal only 20 percent. Most of the revelation they receive never leaves the prayer closet. As partners with God, intercessors are in a place of hiddenness. They must depend upon the Holy Spirit for discernment for what, how much, and when to share."[2]

Pastor, you should not take offense or take it personally when the watchmen (your intercessors) warn you regarding a threat from without or within. The watchmen are commanded to sound the alarm. (See Ezekiel 33:6-7.) They are only attempting to do their job. This only adds to the point that wise pastors will provide training and an appropriate system of communication for the people of prayer in their churches.

A Matter of Life and Death

Intercession is serious business. Spiritual warfare prayer is real war, which presents very real dangers! In the Old Testament, for watchmen to neglect to give warning when they sensed approaching danger, was treasonous and punishable by death. (See Ezekiel 33:6.)

Isaiah writes of the incompetent watchmen of his day, *"His watchmen are blind, they are all ignorant; they are all dumb dogs, they cannot bark; sleeping, lying down, loving to slumber"* (Isaiah 56:10). Until recently this passage from Ezekiel was true for the United States. But we are blessed to say that America's intercessors are waking up to the privilege of prayer.

Intercessory watchmen should realize that their assignment is sometimes a matter of life and death. This is illustrated in my (Eddie) book *Help! I'm Married to an Intercessor*.

> "One morning my wife, Alice, went shopping for building supplies for a project I was working on. Being an intercessor and not a construction worker, she was largely unfamiliar with these items and spent a considerable amount of time in the hardware store looking for them.
>
> Alice was finally standing in the checkout line when, suddenly, she had a brief vision. In her mind's eye—a closed vision—she

saw a man standing in my office pointing a gun at me.

Immediately she grabbed her purse, abandoned her cart with the items she had worked so hard to find, and ran to the car. Alice began to intercede, even as she drove home. Once home, she rushed inside to her prayer closet, where she began crying out to the Lord.

She has since been asked, 'Alice, why didn't you call the office and ask if he was alright?'

'It was time to pray, not take a survey,' she replies.

Alice prayed for 45 minutes until the burden and the sense of urgency subsided. Only then did she call the office and ask, 'Eddie, are you okay?'

'Yeah, fine.' I answered. 'Why do you ask?'

She told me about her vision and how she had entered into prayer.

'Oh that,' I explained. 'He just got saved.'

That morning I had had a counseling session with a medical doctor who was in ill health, separated from his wife, addicted to narcotics and suicidal. After I led him to Christ—and through some significant deliverance—he explained how he had loaded a pistol that morning and placed it on his kitchen counter, intending to bring it to my office and first kill me, then himself. For some 'unexplained reason,' he absentmindedly left the pistol on the kitchen counter.

> Yes, being married to an intercessor definitely has its advantages!"[3]

Even as Alice was assigned as a watchman for my life that day, it is interesting to see where the ancient watchmen were assigned.

⋄ Some were stationed in the watchtowers as lookouts or sentries *on the city walls.* Intercessors have strategic assignments in their prayer closets. From there, they can scour "the spiritual horizon" like air traffic controllers. They often sense spiritual things discerning the good from the bad, the welcome from the unwelcome. In prayer, God sometimes exposes the enemy's plans and shows the intercessor "the cards that Satan is holding." (See Isaiah 62:6; Jeremiah 51:12.)

⋄ They were stationed *around the temple.* Today, more and more churches are making prayer their priority, building prayer rooms, hiring pastors of prayer or enlisting volunteer prayer coordinators. Pastors are identifying and employing their intercessors as their full ministry partners.

Praying around the clock, before and during the worship services reflect the stationing of intercessors around the temple. (See 2 Kings 11:6.)

⋄ They were also stationed *in the streets.* At night, watchmen patrolled the streets of the cities preserving order. We are living in a day when God is calling intercessors into the streets.

By establishing our homes as neighborhood houses of prayer (Lighthouses), and by prayerwalking our streets and praying over each home, school, church and business in our neighborhoods, we are taking our cities back from the dominion of Satan. (See Psalms 127:1; Song of Solomon 3:3, 5:7.)

America is suffering a plague of her own wickedness. The Children of Israel were plagued in Numbers 16:46-48. So, Moses said unto Aaron, *"Take a censer, and put fire therein from off the altar, and put on incense, and go quickly unto the congrega-*

tion, and make an atonement for them: for there is wrath gone out from the LORD; the <u>plague</u> is begun." In Revelation 5:8 we see that incense is a symbol of intercessory prayer.

"And Aaron took it, as Moses commanded, and ran into the midst of the congregation; and, behold, the <u>plague</u> was begun among the people: and he put on incense, and made an atonement for the people. And he stood between the dead and the living; and the <u>plague</u> was stayed."

As Aaron, the High Priest took prayer to the streets *where the people were dying,* the plague was stopped. Lives were saved! It took a radical act on Aaron's part and we too must learn to be instant to obey. As 1 Peter 2:9 teaches, we are today's spiritual priesthood.

Prayerwalking is the act of taking prayer into the streets. Prayerwalking is effective because when standing on the sidewalk, in front of the home, school, or business for which you are praying, you can often pray with more discernment and passion.

Pastor, your intercessors love to take to the streets to repent and pray on site where past wickedness, trauma, bloodshed and broken covenants have been committed. As priests before God they will stand in the gap for the defiled land. It is their calling…their passion.

As prayer teams journey to spiritually troubled sites around the world to pray, many churches are adding financial support for them in their mission's budget. You might consider doing this too.

The four *Praying Through the 10/40 Window* campaigns that began in 1993 focused on this kind of strategic warfare praying. Christians around the world prayed fervent, synchronized prayers for the 65 mostly Muslim, unreached nations between the 10th and the 40th parallels North, between Spain and Japan.

Today books report the miraculous results of these international prayerwalks. As a result of hundreds of prayer journeys, during which thousands of intercessory watchmen prayed on site with insight, these prayed-for nations are experiencing unprecedented moves of God. To effectively pastor intercessors, you must envision them, provide for their training and release them to meaningful ministry like the one mentioned above.

GateKeepers

The gatekeepers or (porters) of the ancient cities were responsible for opening and closing the gates. Pastor, you are a spiritual gatekeeper necessary for providing protection and oversight of the spiritual gates of your city. You have the spiritual influence to either permit or remit situations. What you allow in your own life, and in the life of your congregation, will enable or disable the city church.

Perhaps you have sought to blame others for the problems in your church. Ask the Lord now to reveal anything in your own heart that enables the problem. Remember the words to the old spiritual, "It's not my brother, nor my sister, but it's me, Oh Lord, standin' in the need of prayer." Spiritually blind or careless ministers endanger both the church and the society they seek to serve.

Spiritually blind or careless ministers endanger both the church and the society that they seek to serve.

A major hindrance to any work God wants to do in our lives is for us to have an unteachable spirit. Once we stop being teachable, we become judges. Pastoral pride that says, "I know it all and have no need of others," is tragic. Intercessors, who act as though they hear God better than others, bring their own motives into question.

Perhaps the ultimate danger in the life of a pastor is *pastoral passivity*. Hiding one's head in the sand like an ostrich does not make the problems go away.

Perhaps you've not been offering up prayer for the protection of your. Some pastors have "micro-vision." They are consumed with their own congregations rather than establishing meaningful partnerships with other pastors in order to transform the city to which God has called them.

If this is true of you, ask the Lord Jesus to forgive you for setting your sights too small. Ask him to show you his heart for your city, then take action.

The Nehemiah Anointing

When the ancient walls were devastated by war, God would eventually commission someone to rebuild them. Both Israel and Judah had kings who distinguished themselves as fortifiers, or re-builders of cities. They had "the Nehemiah anointing."

God is presently raising up women and men of vision, who possess the Nehemiah anointing to rebuild the walls of their cities. Oswald Chambers describes vision in his book *My Utmost for His Highest* by saying, "The only way to be obedient to the heavenly vision is to give our utmost for God's highest, and this can only be done by continually and resolutely recalling the vision."[4]

As living stones, when bound by love in proper relationship, we establish an impenetrable spiritual perimeter for our cities. In Katy, Texas, El Paso, Texas, Columbus, Ohio and hundreds of other cities across America and around the world, pastors and churches are meeting regularly across denominational and racial lines for citywide worship and prayer. They are demonstrating that unity (being one) is not synonymous with uniformity (being the same).

God-given diversity strengthens the church. These pastoral gatekeepers and their churches are able to maintain their uniqueness while experiencing unity for the sake of souls. The city church is beginning to demonstrate the levels of Christian unity that will cause the world to believe!

Nothing will be impossible for those who are committed to rebuild the spiritual walls of our cities. Pastors (gatekeepers) and intercessors (watchmen) together must face their common adversary, Satan. He is an ancient deity who has diligently fought to keep this strategic partnership from forming. He will not give up easily. His goal is to divide and conquer. He will do everything he can to erode our relationships and hinder the healing of our cities.

A well-educated pastor with a highly skilled staff, the most innovative programs, supported by the latest technological tools, is no match for Satan and his forces. A pastor (gatekeeper) may have the authority to open and close the gates, but at best he can see little beyond the walls.

On the other hand, gifted, committed intercessors (watchmen) may have the ability to see beyond the walls and discern dangers that are about to befall the city. But they often have limited authority to take appropriate action unless the gatekeeper cooperates with their warning. It is critical that pastors and intercessors be linked together as ministry partners.

"In that day shall this song be sung in the land of Judah;
We have a strong city; salvation will God appoint
for walls and bulwarks"
(Isaiah 26:1).

CHAPTER FIVE

Becoming
A House of Prayer

Is Prayer our Priority?

"My house will be called a house of prayer,
but you are making it a den of robbers"
(Matthew 21:13).

Everyone knows the purpose of a fire house. Everyone knows the specialty food that is served at the International House of Pancakes. But few people know the purpose of the church.

Jesus said that the church he is building is to be a "house of prayer." However, prayer is not the priority of the average church today. At best, prayer is one of a multitude of other church programs.

More often than not, our churches are houses of sports, preaching, or musical pageantry. They are not houses of prayer! In fact, prayer is low on their list of priorities. May we suggest that whatever our churches are, other than houses of prayer, is what *we* have made them.

At noon, when we arrived at the Presidential Hotel in Port Harcourt, Nigeria, we were amazed to see four African businessmen kneeling in prayer on the sidewalk in front of the hotel. We recognized immediately that they were Muslim. But we were taken with their bold commitment to pray. One would rarely, if ever, see four American businessmen kneeling in front of a busy hotel to pray.

One reason revival is coming to Africa is because even before coming to Christ, Africans are praying people. They simply change the direction of their prayers, from false gods to the true God.

When talking one day to prayer leader Ron Gaynor, I (Eddie) referred to Elijah and "the false prophets" of Baal.

Ron interrupted me and said, "Eddie, those weren't false prophets."

"They weren't?" I responded with surprise.

"No," he continued. "They were prophets of a false God. What we should ask ourselves is, are we as passionate and committed to prayer and to loving and trusting our God as they were?"

> We are powerless because we are prayerless!

Imagine that a survey was taken of the 100 homes nearest your church. What percentage of them would characterize it as "the place where people go to pray?" Certainly, the American church is not short on programs or ideas. But we are definitely short on spiritual power. For unlike Peter and John in Acts 3:6, we would be far more apt to say to a cripple today, *"Here is some silver and gold. Sorry, but we don't have the ability to command you to rise up and walk!"* We are powerless because we are prayerless!

Only a praying pastor can develop a praying church! However, study after study indicates that unlike their Korean counterparts (who pray an average of 90 minutes a day), prayer is not the priority of the average American pastor.

- In response to a survey taken at a pastor's conference in Dallas, Texas several years ago, 95% said they spend less than 5 minutes a day in prayer.
- A survey by C. Peter Wagner of 572 American pastors revealed that their average time spent in personal prayer was 22 minutes a day.
- A third survey indicated no appreciable difference in the amount of time spent in prayer between church leaders and average church members. This should not be!

World-famous tenor, Luciano Pavarotti has said, "When I don't practice one day, I know it. When I don't practice two days, my voice teacher knows it. When I don't practice three days, the whole world knows it!" Sadly, we are exposed. It is painfully evident to our world that the American church has yet to become a house of prayer.

Prayer IS the Priority of a House of Prayer!

In the December 1999 issue of *Spirit of Revival* magazine, Sammy Tippit writes,

> "The great need of the hour is that pulpits throughout this land might be filled with humble, holy, praying men. A prayerless pulpit produces a powerless people. Powerless to overcome troubling sins. Powerless to change the culture. Powerless to give witness of their great Savior. And a powerless pew produces a cynical public. The church then becomes the object of disdain, because to a great extent it has lost its authenticity.
>
> In the book of Acts, it is said that the people recognized that those proclaiming the Gospel were 'unlearned and ignorant men,' and 'they marvelled; and they took knowledge of them, that they had been with Jesus' (Acts 4:13). Today, I'm afraid people can easily observe that we have very intelligent and educated preachers but that few of them have been with Jesus. And we wonder why revival tarries.
>
> Recently, a pastor confided to me, "I preach about prayer. But the truth is that it's been a long time since I've had any real quality time in prayer." I don't believe that his situa-

tion is unique. We talk a lot about prayer but pray little. We read books on prayer but do nothing about what we read. We say that prayer is a necessity for victorious Christian living but have scheduled God out of our inner life. We proclaim that prayer should be the priority of the church but never weep because of our empty prayer meetings."[1]

In a house of prayer, prayer is the priority. It is foundational to everything else and to every other ministry. All other ministries are designed to go to men for God. Prayer is the only one that goes to God for men.

Jack Hayford tells how his personal failure as a pastor many years ago led him to desperation. One day he went into his auditorium and began praying over each seat. He did so faithfully and soon the building was full. Through the years, no doubt as a result of his personal commitment to prayer, God has given him an international ministry.

Martin Luther described his prayer life: "In a typical day I am charged with the pastorate of three congregations. I teach regularly at the seminary. I have students living in my house. I am writing three books. Countless people write to me. When I start each day, therefore, I make it a point to spend an hour in prayer with God. But, if I have a particularly busy day and am more rushed than usual, I make it a point to spend two hours with God before I start the day." Now *that's* making prayer *a priority!*

Biblical leaders were all men of prayer. Moses, David, Elijah and Daniel are good examples. In fact, James writes that *"Elijah was a man subject to like passions as we are, and he prayed earnestly that it might not rain: and it rained not on the earth by the space of three years and six months. And he prayed again, and the heaven gave rain, and the earth brought forth her fruit"* (James 5:17-18).

Samuel actually regarded it a sin not to pray. *"God forbid that I should sin against the LORD in ceasing to pray for you"* (1 Samuel 12:23).

Samuel actually regarded it a sin not to pray.

I (Alice) believe the Lord is releasing a new level of leadership anointing in the 21ˢᵗ Century church that I call "the Samuel anointing." I see the Old Testament prophetic priests Eli and his sons Phineas and Hophni as representing the church of the past. (See 1 Samuel chapters 2-4.) Eli was fat, undisciplined and a poor steward of the priesthood. His sons were immoral, arrogant, demanding and unable to perceive the presence of God. They portray what much of the church (the New Testament priesthood) has been. (See Revelation 1:6.)

But God is offering us a new type of leadership *if we will humble ourselves and seek the face of God.* We can have a Samuel anointing. Samuel's reign in Israel established "a new beginning." He was a righteous prophet and judge of Israel. He was an intercessor filled with integrity, honesty and holiness. (See 1 Samuel 12:1-5.) He never oppressed the poor or took the best of the offerings, as Eli had done. I believe it pleases the Lord to grant this Samuel anointing to those who will respond to God's conditions of humility and prayer.

Jesus, our Lord and our example, would often withdraw to a lonely place and pray. He would sometimes slip away for predawn prayer. His life proved that prayer was his highest priority! Of all the miraculous things his disciples saw him do, the one thing they wanted Jesus to teach them was how to pray as he prayed. (See Luke 11:1.) Perhaps they knew that his prayer life was the key to his power!

Undoubtedly they learned and practiced Christ's secret. For the Book of Acts records that the early New Testament church did the same works that Jesus did.

E.M. Bounds in his book *The Weapon of Prayer*, goes as far as to say,

"The thing far above other things in the equipment of the preacher is prayer. Before everything else he must be a person who makes a specialty of prayer. A prayerless preacher is a misnomer. He has either missed his calling, or he has grievously failed God, who called him into the ministry."[2]

The Heart of a House of Prayer

Someone has said, "The person who knows *how* will always work for the person who knows *why*." As we have interviewed intercessors (people of prayer) and examined churches that are becoming houses of prayer, we have discovered that in both cases, *they know why!*

Members of a house of prayer know how prayer fits into their personal relationship with God and into the purposes of God. The Christians are committed to prayer as a life-style. Pastor, you don't get people to pray at church. You enable *pray-ers* to pray at church.

Too many church members assume that since God is both all knowing and all-powerful, there is no point in praying. They reason if it's God's will for something to happen, it will happen regardless of what we do.

◇ James argues against this when he writes, *"Yet you do not have because you do not ask"* (James 4:2 NKJV).

◇ Joshua's experience argued against this when he experienced victory as long as Aaron and Hur held Moses' arms up, and defeat when they failed to do so. (See Exodus 17:10-13.)

◇ Jesus taught that persistent prayer produces consistent results. Implicit in that verse is that our failure to pray produces nothing. (See Luke 11:5-9.)

Weak praying makes weak churches. Years ago we attended a large convention. Returning early from a lunch

Weak praying makes weak churches.

break, we found the lights out in the large city auditorium. As we felt our way through the cavernous darkness we almost tripped over something on the floor. On second look we discovered that it was not something, but rather someone. It was famous author and preacher Dr. R. G. Lee, pastor of Bellevue Baptist Church, Memphis, Tennessee. He was to be the featured speaker in the afternoon session. There he was, groaning in prayer all alone, face down on the floor in front of the speaker's platform. We reverently side stepped him and quietly made our way to the nearest exit. Two young ministers stopped us as we walked out into the brightly lit hallway. One asked, "Sir, can you tell us how to get the power turned on in the auditorium?"

Pointing back at the figure on the floor of the darkened hall I (Eddie) replied, "No, but I believe Dr. Lee knows how to get the power turned on!"

If the fervent prayer of a righteous person accomplishes much (see James 5:16), then the prayerlessness of a righteous person leaves people, places and things unchanged. So prayerlessness at least means no change for the better, and sometimes it spells disaster.

In Ezekiel 22:30-31 Israel had sinned and deserved to be punished. God, wanting to extend mercy to them, looked for someone who would stand in the gap. He was looking for someone who would pray as Habakkuk prayed, *"O LORD, I have heard your speech and was afraid; O LORD, revive your work in the midst of the years! In the midst of the years make it known; In wrath remember mercy"* (Habakkuk 3:2). Finding no one willing to pray, he poured out his wrath upon the nation.

The Power of Prayer

A church that is truly a house of prayer knows that God has chosen to move in response to prayer. These unique people know that prayer…

1. Releases the ministry of angels. (See Daniel 10.)
2. Puts the power of God into the work of God, and
3. Accesses the presence of God!

Intercessors know that God rules the world through the prayers of his people. (See Exodus 33:11-23; John 15:7; James 5:15-16; 1 John 5:14-15.) This elevates our prayers to a position of highest significance in the economy of God. It makes us co-laborers with him in this world. God wants to partner with us not because he is dependent upon us. But because it is the way he has chosen to exercise his will.

> As John Wesley said, "God does nothing but in answer to prayer."

In the Garden of Eden man was given dominion over the earth. But Adam lost his authority to Satan. Jesus, the Second Adam, retrieved it and has given dominion over the earth back to man. As John Wesley said, "God does nothing but in answer to prayer."

A pastor told me (Eddie) that he wanted his church to become a house of prayer. I told him, "Pastor, you might not want that."

"Why?" He asked.

"Because," I explained, "prayer will then be your church's highest priority. It will mean that your church will be spending the larger amount of its time and money on prayer.

Your Sunday morning worship service, the jewel in the setting of your church's schedule, will become a corporate prayer meeting."

"Whoa! We can't do all of that!" He exclaimed.

"Then you are going to have to get with God and discover what he does require of you."

He returned a few days later with the new prayer strategy that God had given him.

Prayer Strategies

Strategies that various pastors have applied to move their churches toward becoming houses of prayer include:

⋄ *Pastors are setting an example by setting aside one day a week for a personal, private prayer retreat.* The pastor is not available on those days for any other business or activity. His secretary and staff protect him in this endeavor. Pastors doing this report that this weekly prayer day produces clearer direction for the church and personal power for their preaching.

⋄ *Pastors are establishing a personal prayer shield for themselves, their families and their churches.* Pastor, ask the Lord to identify intercessors in your church who have been commissioned by him to pray for you and your family.

⋄ *Pastors are setting aside weekly half-day staff prayer meetings.* Tuesday morning 9:00 AM – Noon works well in some cases. This brings staff unity and interdependence. It reduces isolation in ministry and the "Lone Ranger mentality." It also serves as a constant reminder to the staff that every facet of their work and ministry is dependent upon the Holy Spirit and prayer.

⋄ *Pastors are allowing for meaningful times of prayer in the worship services.* Some are planning a time of corporate prayer, during which two or three intercessors are selected ahead of time to come to the microphone to lead in prayer.

Many churches observe a time during the worship service when those with needs are invited to come to the altar for personal prayer ministry. The intercessors and others are selected, trained and released to serve as altar ministers.

- *Still other churches have intercessors stationed in the prayer room to pray during each worship service.* Three or four people are enough and the intercessors rotate so the weight is not on the same people each week.

- *Prayer becomes a significant part of every meeting.* Whether it is a Sunday School class, a home cell group meeting, a church picnic, a deacon's meeting or some other committee or team meeting, an intentional time of extended intercessory prayer is replacing the obligatory "closing word of prayer."

- *Prayer will be taught and exercised by everyone from the womb to the tomb.* Nursery workers will pray over the children in their care. Preschoolers through senior adults will be taught and be given opportunities to practice meaningful prayer. Young children are sometimes taken into the adult classes to pray for individual adults. This teaches young children the importance of prayer. It is amazing to see how powerfully God touches the adults as these young people pray.

- *Training in prayer and intercession.* There will be seminars and conferences from time to time throughout the year to teach the congregation to pray. Pastor, it is crucial that you attend the prayer conferences that come to your church. Your people will do what you do, not what you say. The moment you delegate the modeling of prayer to a staff member or lay leader, you've ceased leading a house of prayer.

- *Prayer chains are developed and utilized, including the use of teleconference-type calls via 3-way phone calls.* Prayer chains may include a sign-up sheet for every 30 minutes or hour. The person finishing one slot telephones the next person in line thus "passing the prayer torch."

In one church in Atlanta, Georgia, every adult church member has the 3-way dialing option on their home phone. They partner with two others in prayer triplets. Prayer requests appear in the church bulletin each Sunday morning. At an appointed time during the week, the members place their 3-way calls and pray together over the phone for the prayer assignments.

Another church's prayer chain has people coming to the church throughout a 24-hour period. In some cases, paid security is present during the night hours. Many Southern Baptists have Watchmen Prayer Ministries in which they establish a prayer wall of 168 hours. (There are 168 hours in a week.) Once they complete one 168 hour wall, many start another.

◇ *Special prayer emphases are offered.* (See Appendix C)
◇ *Local churches are building special facilities for prayer.* Church prayer rooms are being built in record numbers. The World Prayer Center, coordinated by C. Peter Wagner in Colorado Springs, Colorado is networking 2,000 church prayer rooms electronically to coordinate prayer for critical issues. The Jericho Center, coordinated by Dick Eastman, Every Home for Christ in Colorado Springs, Colorado, will soon feature 24-hour prayer and praise rooms! Mike Bickle coordinates the Tabernacle of David in Kansas City, Missouri. It is a ministry of continuous prayer and praise.
◇ *Pastors are staffing for prayer.* More and more churches across America are adding a Prayer Pastor to their staff or recruiting a layperson to coordinate the church's prayer ministry.

It's a Dumb Idea

A man came to me (Eddie) awhile back saying, "My pastor has asked me to become our church's prayer coordinator. I invited you to lunch so you could tell me what I should do."

With my usual dry humor I smiled and said, "Go back and resign."

Somewhat taken aback he asked, "Resign? But why?"

"Well," I went on to explain, "it's a dumb idea."

"What do you mean?" He asked, still confused.

I continued methodically, "More than likely your pastor wants you to take the church membership directory and divide the names into prayer teams of fifteen. Then select a prayer captain over each team and a prayer coordinator over a group of three captains."

Suddenly, he began frantically searching for something. "Wait a minute. What are you doing?" I asked.

"Trying to find my pen so I can write all this down," he quickly answered.

"Don't write this down!" I playfully scolded him. "I've already told you it's a dumb idea! That's not prayer ministry! That's multilevel marketing! You'll not be a pastor of prayer, you'll be a manager of unmotivated people. You'll spend all your time looking for people to fill the slots!"

In the '70s we tried motivating people to pray using guilt and shame. We quoted Scriptures "against them," admonishing and pleading for their attendance. We whined, "Please show up Wednesday night. I really need for you to be here. Don't let me down."

In the '80s we tried motivating our members with fear. With intimidation we showed them the evil at hand and warned them to pray. Still our least-attended services were those that included prayer.

At the start of the decade of the '90s, God "jump-started" his praying people around the world! He also began answering prayer. In fact, the best way to encourage people to pray today is to identify those the Lord is mobilizing, affirm them, equip them and report to them all the ways God is answering their prayer and then get out of their way!

I told my lunch partner, "Go back and tell your pastor that you will pastor the praying people in your church. Then conduct a survey or offer a spiritual gifts test. C. Peter Wagner has a great spiritual gifts test in his book, *Spiritual Gifts Can Help Your Church Grow*, published by Regal Books. Once you discover who your praying people are, then enlist them. You may have 350 church members and only 35 intercessors.

You'll discover that, like rabbits, they will multiply!

Tell your pastor that you will lead and train those 35 people. Then pour your heart and life into the newly recruited intercessors as you equip them for the work of the ministry (see Ephesians 4:11-13). You'll soon discover that, like rabbits, they will multiply!"

Pastor, your intercessors are looking for models and mentors. They want instruction in prayer, along with the support, understanding and encouragement of their pastors. People who pray are looking for love and affection attached to the security of discipline and instruction.

As you provide church-wide prayer opportunities, we encourage you to invest yourself in the gifted pray-ers that God has placed in your charge. Pastors everywhere are beginning to realize that in the past they have spent too much time trying to mobilize the 90% of their members who rarely pray, and too little time pastoring the 10% of their people who love to pray. This is like parents who neglect their good child, so they can correct their bad one. Face it. You are never going to motivate all of your members to be prayer warriors.

In Conclusion

The transitioning of a church into a house of prayer should be done slowly. Care should be given when challenging the slow adapters in your congregation. They need time to adjust to change.

Concsider preaching a series of sermons on prayer. Prepare a recommended list of books for your people to read. (See Appendix B.) Chart the path toward becoming a house of prayer with exciting programs, posters, videos and prayer calendars.

Your goals should not exceed your manpower (your leadership potential) or your available time. It takes time to turn a big ship. Impatient leaders can "sink" ships. Sometimes, they themselves are thrown overboard. Be patient in the process. There are three important foci to consider when developing your prayer programs.

⬦ *OUTWARD FOCUS.* A house of prayer should have an outward focus. Churches often direct their prayer at their needs alone. Many Wednesday evening prayer meetings are reduced to praying for the sick, leaving the group discouraged by all the needs.

It's okay to pray for the needs of your church, but you need to pray strategic prayers for the lost. We believe God is challenging churches to move prayer outside the four walls and begin to pray prayers that change the climate of the cities. We must pray for revival and spiritual awakening as I (Alice) describe in Ted Haggard and Jack Hayford's book *Loving Your City Into the Kingdom!*

> "October 30, 1990, is a night to remember. A historic moment occurred as Houston-area pastors and churches gathered in the coliseum to pray for revival and spiritual awakening. The event, called 'Breakthrough Houston,' involved dozens of churches representing various denominations and ethnic groups.

For several months committees met, pastors prayed and plans were laid for the special event. The cooperating churches and parachurch ministries participated in a three-day 'PowerFast' leading up to Tuesday night. At dusk, thousands of Houstonians emerged from the underground parking areas and filed their way into the coliseum.

Christians from many denominations and worship styles burst into the huge auditorium filled with joyous praise. Pastors, charismatic and non-charismatic, evangelical and liturgical, first met backstage for prayer; and then made their way to seats on the giant stage. The atmosphere was electric.

The program consisted of a blending of praise and worship and intercession. Between the times of worship, pastors were assigned to speak briefly and pray for various subjects. Corporately the city's Church in Houston repented for its sin.

We repented for our personal sins. We prayed prayers of replacement, asking God to replace the spirit of pride with a spirit of humility; the spirit of racism with a spirit of acceptance; the spirit of anger and violence with a spirit of peace.

We prayed petitionary prayers for pastors and churches, children and homes, schools and universities, businesses and industry. We earnestly cried out for God to break the cycle of crime in our city. As each worship set finished and each prayer was completed, the corporate spirit grew with intensity.

Each person was given a prayer covenant and a corporate declaration we were to announce to principalities above the city. Around 8:45 P.M., we read the covenant of unity and prayer in unison. Then authoritatively, we read the declaration to break the power of the enemy over Houston. The coliseum seemed to tremble, as the shout of thousands of Christians roared heavenward! We all had a sense that somehow spiritual strongholds had been broken. However, having only a subjective opinion of our supposed breakthrough, objective facts were needed to prove our discerned opinion. So we asked the Lord for confirmation. We concluded the evening by taking communion together.

Two days later, on November 1, a news report entitled 'What Were Those Lights in the Sky?' appeared in the *Houston Chronicle* on page 28A. The article read as follows:

'According to some accounts, it definitely was a burning aircraft that crashed and exploded in the Tomball (Northwest Houston) area.... It was the stuff of an unsolved Halloween mystery, but authorities agreed that the UFO sighted in northwest Harris County and southwest Montgomery County on Tuesday night probably resulted from a meteor shower. Still, area law enforcement agencies, as well as fire stations, had no choice but to take the reports that came in about 8:45 P.M. seriously.'

To those of us who had participated in Breakthrough Houston, this was a confirming sign in the heavenlies. However, further confirmation was to be noted.

From that night, crime in the city of Houston began to decrease. In December 1994, the *Houston Post* reported that violent crime had dropped 29.2 percent since January 1991. By 1995, the *Houston Chronicle* reported crime had dropped an additional 31.9 percent to a record decrease of 51.5 percent. This level has been maintained during the first six months of 1996."[3]

Houston is still experiencing record-breaking reductions in crime. The reason? Pastors are praying together and intercessors are prayerwalking neighborhoods, and both pastors and intercessors are working together.

◊ *INWARD FOCUS*. The ministry of a house of prayer should have an inward focus as well. Imbalance happens when churches focus their prayer on the city to the neglect of the needs of the congregation and church staff. Never get so outward focused that the needs of your church are overlooked! Equip some of your church members to offer personal prayer ministry to people who are hurting or sick. Most Christians in our churches state that they have never been personally ministered to through prayer.

◊ *UPWARD FOCUS*. The ministry of a house of prayer should have an upward focus. Prayer is part of our priestly ministry as believers. It has to do with our own personal intimate relationship with the Father. It is not a mere tool to get things done. It is a doorway into the presence of our Father. Be careful. Teach your people that a close, intimate relationship with Jesus is the key to a fruitful and happy life. Suggest prayer books or daily devotional materials that aid a novice in their private prayer time.

Alvin VanderGriend, coordinator of Houses of Prayer Everywhere in Grand Rapids, reports that a church in Phoenix, Arizona randomly selected 160 homes from the telephone directory. They divided it into two groups. For ninety days the Phoenix church prayed for 80 of the homes, and the other 80 homes where not prayed for.

At the end of the 90 days they called each of the 160 homes, identified themselves and asked for permission to drop by and pray for the family and any needs they might have. Over the phone they explained that they were not prospecting for their church and they were not asking to come in.

Of the 80 homes for which they had not prayed, only one invited them to come by. Of the 80 prayed-for homes, 69 invited them to come by. When they did, 45 homeowners invited them inside to pray. Wow! The power of prayer is dramatically seen in these results!

Pastor, you too might see these kinds of results if you will get your intercessors connected to your vision. We believe that intercessors are helpful in transitioning a church into a "house of prayer."

⋄ Praying people believe in the importance of prayer. It is their focus.

⋄ They will be quickest to pray and will usually pray the most often.

⋄ They experience the intercessory anointing the most often, which inspires others to pray.

⋄ They will be pacesetters and models for the rest of the church.

A pastor determined to see his church become a house of prayer, will learn how to disciple and encourage his intercessors well. In the next chapter we will discover what intercessors need from their pastors.

CHAPTER SIX

Understanding Intercessors

Intercessory people are often called "prayer warriors." Our friend, the late Dr. Mickey Bonner would say, "A prayer warrior is the person a wimp calls in the time of trouble." This is because the ministry of prayer, which is an appeal to the Father, is also an assault against the forces of darkness.

Intercessors, especially *warfare intercessors* are probably the most difficult to understand. Many don't even understand themselves. They tend to be the more controversial intercessors because many have an ability to discern the spiritual realm. The American church has embraced what missiologists call "the excluded middle." We believe in the third heaven where God is and the physical heavens that we can see. But we ignore the second heaven where Scripture teaches that Satan, the prince of the power of the air, principalities, powers and rulers of the darkness of this world reside. (See Ephesians 2:2; 6:12.) As a result, warfare intercessors are often discredited, ignored and especially wounded by misinformed and/or insensitive church leaders. Over time, these crippled warriors become defensive, aloof and unteachable if left without loving support.

Pastor, let us say it clearly. There are prayer warriors in your church. Either you will teach them how to fight for your vision, or they will fight for theirs or someone else's. They are fighters at heart! These tenacious, militant people will fight with or without you! It's your choice. Mark it down, there will come a time, as the "bullets" of accusation, fear or lies come against your ministry, when you will need a warfare intercessor. I (Alice) am a fighter in prayer. Prayer assignments that require decades to pray through will be abandoned years earlier by those in the body of Christ who refuse to fight in prayer. Thank God for warfare intercessors who, like "spiritual bulldogs," are unwilling to let go of tough assignments. Let's not overlook the need for this type of intercessor. But the schism must be addressed if we are to see cooperation in the future.

However, much of the time pastors and intercessors are intimidated and threatened by each other. Jonathan Benz, pastor and outreach director for Covenant Centre International in Palm Beach Gardens, Florida wrote an article in *Ministries Today* on pastoring intercessors. Jonathan agrees with us when he says, "Far too often pastors and intercessors have an adversarial relationship rather than one of mutuality, support and respect."[1]

Maturity versus Immaturity

Most of the following characteristics could be applied to any Christian. Here, however, we apply them to the intercessor.

⬧ *Patience is a mark of the maturing intercessor.* Faithfully trusting God in all things while waiting for multiple confirmations requires great patience. Maturing intercessors are *led* not *driven* by the revelation they receive. They exercise caution and submit themselves and their revelations to multiple counselors. (See Deuteronomy 19:15 and Proverbs 24:6.)

Seasoned intercessors realize that diagnosis does not mean assignment!

Immature intercessors tend to be impatient with revelations they receive from the Lord. Everything can appear to be *an emergency*. When this happens, their panic and apprehension can alarm others also. The critical issue of revelatory *timing* is a learned skill.

◇ *Seasoned intercessors are full of faith.* Knowing the difference between faith and presumption, these intercessors usually refuse to move presumptuously into battle. They count the costs and wait for specific instructions from the Lord. A wise intercessor seeks the advice of pastoral leadership to confirm the Lord's direction and is not threatened by delays. *"For which of you, intending to build a tower, does not sit down first and count the cost, whether he has enough to finish it lest, after he has laid the foundation, and is not able to finish, all who see it begin to mock him, saying, 'This man began to build and was not able to finish.'"* (Luke 14:28-30).

Knowing what is wrong and even knowing the solution to it, does not constitute an order from God to take action. Like Jesus, intercessors should only say and do what they hear the Father saying and doing. (See John 5:19.)

Unseasoned intercessors, on the other hand, are often presumptuous. They'll charge hell with a water pistol! They confuse boldness with bravado and faith with presumption! As their pastor you should lovingly point out their need for balance and confirmations.

Prayer journey leader, some intercessors may neither be prepared nor qualified to engage in a warfare-related prayer journey. And it would be wrong for you to issue a blanket invitation that might involve those who could suffer a serious setback as a result of their participation. Here are a few ground rules that should be observed.

> • If you are inviting people to be part of a prayer journey team who are not from your own church, then have them submit a *Pastoral/ Church Covenant for Prayer Journey Participants* form. (See Appendix D. You'll also find our *Personal Covenant* and *Personal Information* forms for use on prayer journey assignments.)

- If you are planning to involve intercessors from your own church, make sure your pastor approves of their participation.
- If you are unsure about taking someone on your prayer assignment, then follow the urging of your spirit (see Colossians 3:15) and lovingly encourage them to wait for a future trip.

◇ *Well-adjusted intercessors are able to discern between the natural and the spiritual.* They are not "religious" people. Rather, they are delightfully *genuine* people who are practical in their Christian walk. You might say they are *supernaturally natural.*

Others love being with them. One reason might be because they esteem others better than themselves. (See Philippians 2:3.)

Maladjusted intercessors on the other hand are spiritually weird. They are prone to spiritualize everything. I (Eddie) assure you, it's not a "blonde" thing...not even a female thing. Gentlemen intercessors who refuse to be accountable to spiritual authority can "weird out" like anyone else!

I (Alice) was embarrassed at a recent Prayer & Fasting meeting in Houston when I saw an intercessor enter the meeting *intentionally* dressed in dirty rags with ash rubbed on her face. Perhaps it would have been alright had this been a one-time act of obedience to the Lord, but this intercessor has a reputation in Houston for "weirdness." Intercessors—don't embarrass the rest of us! Some of *what you think is God...*isn't! Get confirmation from at least two or three key intercessory leaders before you act out unusual behaviors. *Please!*

To focus more on the demonic than on the Lord is unhealthy. It is difficult for some to accept the fact that we live in a fallen world and each of us has a lower nature. Some people of prayer don't seem to realize that sin is something against which we will all struggle until we leave this earth whether we encounter the demonic or not. It's easier to blame the devil for everything!

Intercessors may find it difficult to quietly hold the revelation received as a sacred trust, as Jesus' mother Mary did after the angel spoke to her (see Luke 2:19). For example, an intercessor, regardless of gender, who feels that God has shown them prophetic glimpses of the future, may want others to see it. They become frustrated when others don't.

> The enemy is always ready to speak to you, so beware lest the devil discredit you.

When their pastor fails to see their prophetic insight, they may assume that he is disinterested, or worse yet, spiritually inadequate. In fact, if the pastor fails to see or sense the revelation, it may simply be a result of the differences in their spiritual gifting.

Because of what intercessors see, they tend to focus on the battle and the victory, and fail to consider the potential costs. Pastors, on the other hand, tend to focus on the safety of the sheep. They *do* count the costs. A true shepherd wants not only to win battles, but also to protect people in the process. If at all possible, he wants to prevent casualties in the skirmish. Mature intercessors will understand the pastor's heart and will try to work *with* him, not *around* him.

⋄ *Balanced intercessors don't push or promote their revelations.* Although they hear God's voice more clearly and more often than most of us, mature intercessors rarely mention what they've heard. They hold what they hear loosely and consider it a sacred trust. Thoughtful intercessors neither manipulate nor monopolize others with what they feel the Lord has said to them.

Unbalanced intercessors are sometimes known for much speaking. Speaking of their revelations, they will sometimes explain that others "are just not mature enough to hear the truth." Such prideful attitudes lead to self-promotion. We must all learn to live, to speak and to minister at the level of God's promotion. (See Psalm 75:6-7.)

Some of us have inadvertently put pressure upon intercessors. We have a pastor friend who always greets us with, "Do you have a word for me today?" Constantly seeking God's revelation *from* others can result in deception. Our intercessors are not God's version of the psychic hotline!

Another tendency for inexperienced intercessors is to let their intercession degenerate to an attempt to "get a word" for their pastor. Dear intercessor, if "getting a word" ever becomes the focus of your prayer-life, you are in danger of being misled. Spiritual discernment and spiritual pride live next door to each other. It is easy for someone who hears from God routinely and fairly accurately to slip into spiritual pride and presumption. God will not be pressured into speaking to you. The enemy is always ready to speak to you, so beware lest the devil discredit you. The Lord *occasionally* mentions us to our intercessors while they are praying. But we are especially grateful to know that they *regularly* mention us to him.

Intercessors need to know that it is God alone who establishes their credibility. It is evidenced neither by the accuracy nor the amount of their revelation but by their character. Rather than let the revelation prompt them to prayer, the revelation can provoke immature intercessors to manipulate people and situations. It is never proper to flaunt one's spiritual gifts or to draw attention to oneself.

While it is true that many prophetically gifted intercessors often hear God, unbalanced intercessors seeking acceptance from others will sometimes exaggerate this ability. Prophetic gifts can lead to spiritual pride and to legalism.

One warfare intercessor calling to share an experience with me (Eddie) said, "Then the Lord *gave me* a word of knowledge that so and so, and such and such had happened."

A few minutes after our conversation she called again. This time she called to apologize. "It was my husband that the Lord spoke that word to, not to me. I am so sorry I lied. Why did I exaggerate like that?" She asked.

Quickly answering herself she said, "I did that to protect my pride." Don't we all protect our pride from time to time? Of course we do. How refreshing to see a brother or a sister who is quick to repent and willing to walk at such a level of accountability.

◇ *Experienced intercessors are often prayer strategists.* God-given authority is based on maturity. (See Psalm 75:2.) These intercessors let God establish the platform and choose the appointed time for them to speak. It was said of Samuel, *"The Lord was with Samuel as he grew up, and he let none of his words fall to the ground. And all Israel from Dan to Beersheba recognized that Samuel was attested by the Lord"* (1 Samuel 3:19-20).

Inexperienced intercessors sometimes seek to be heard, to be out front, to have a position of leadership or to at least be close to a person of authority. Many leaders are actually being used by those misguided souls who are attracted to leadership.

◇ *Sincere intercessors typically recognize God's authority and work with it, not against it.* They have humble and teachable hearts. They pray for, speak well of, and support their pastors, husbands and others in authority. They wouldn't dream of seeking to control their pastors.

Because they are Kingdom-minded, these intercessors are willing to partner with other groups and congregations, but keep their *roots of accountability* planted firmly in their local church and its leadership.

These intercessors desire to grow in the areas of prayer and find security in the accountability process. They love to "be pastored."

Insincere intercessors find it difficult to submit to authority, any authority not just pastoral authority. Some women, for example, have dysfunctional relationships with their fathers, bosses, and/or husbands and whether intentionally or unintentionally they continually attempt to control or to correct them. Similarly, some men suffer dysfunctional relationships with their mothers, female bosses, and/or wives. They feel threatened by any articulate, skillful woman in authority. So whether intentionally or unintentionally, they continually dishonor women, suppressing their opinions and excluding them in conversation.

Intercessors who refuse to be accountable are the most dangerous as they flit from group to group, congregation to congregation like spiritual butterflies. When challenged they explain it is because they love people or that no one congregation or pastor understands them and can meet their personal needs. Quite often the truth is that their pastor *does* understand them. This intercessor refuses to become a meaningful member of a single church in order to avoid being held accountable for ministry decisions and activities. Moving around provides a greater audience, showing the intercessor greater attention and providing an opportunity to influence a greater number of people.

These people are apt to say, "I am not submitted to man, I am submitted to God alone," which being interpreted means, "I am not spiritually accountable at all." It is God who establishes spiritual authority. He does so through his church. God establishes and uses human authority. Failure to submit to God-ordained human authority is failure to submit to God. (See Romans 13:1-2.) If your pastor is only your pastor when you think he's right, then he's not your pastor at all. He's only a consultant.

To avoid accountability, some intercessors resort to the "lone ranger" syndrome. They act as though the rest of the body is not capable or worthy of having a meaningful relationship with them. Many do this because of past hurts or present bitterness. In all fairness, the Lord does give us the assignment to be alone at times, but only briefly as seen in the life of Christ, and never a life-style of alienation.

◇ *Disciplined intercessors know and love the Scripture. They never elevate personal revelation above the Word of God.* These brothers and sisters have committed large portions of Scripture to memory. They are never threatened when asked to submit their revelations to God's Word, knowing that God never writes one thing and speaks another. In fact, it is said of God's prophet Samuel, who was familiar with the audible voice of God, *"The Lord continued to appear at Shiloh, and there he revealed himself to Samuel through his word"* (1 Samuel 3:21).

> Sadly, some intercessors know God in the context of war, but not in the context of intimacy!

In contrast, undisciplined intercessors are frequently not grounded in God's Word. By elevating what they think they've heard from God above God's Word, they endanger themselves and others.

◇ *Well-trained intercessors focus on the Lord Jesus.* The enemy gets no more time, energy and attention from a well-trained intercessor than is absolutely necessary to complete her assignment.

Although I (Eddie) love singing warfare songs and have written many, there is a subtle danger of our allowing warfare to replace worship. Just as a pastor's study can replace his devotional life, warfare praying, with its excitement, can also replace an intercessor's devotional prayer life. Sadly, some intercessors know God in the context of war, but not in the context of intimacy! It is sad because the level of our spiritual authority is directly related to the level of our intimacy with the Father.

Poorly trained intercessors focus on the enemy for extended periods gravitating toward spiritual superstition, which is demonic deception.

A man came to me (Eddie) for counseling one morning. He said, "Last night my wife and I were almost asleep when she slapped me across the chest and shouted, 'Charles, wake up! Oh my God, we forgot to pray for the kids!' What's wrong with this, Brother Eddie?"

I said, "Charles, your wife is superstitious. She thinks God protects your children only because you pray for them."

"Doesn't he?" He asked.

"No," I explained. "He protects your children because they are yours and you are his." Prayer is a privilege God extends to us in our relationship to him. Isn't it comforting to know that Jesus Christ ever lives to intercede for our kids even when we don't?

◇ *Godly intercessors love people.* They are not critical, judgmental, or superstitious, but have a unique ability to show incredible grace and mercy. We have found that spiritually mature intercessors are loving, gracious and faithful servants of the Lord who never elevate their prayer ministry above people. Bobbye Byerly, prayer coordinator for the World Prayer Center in Colorado Springs, is one of the most godly women we know. She is always filled with joy and even though her schedule is tight Bobbye always has time for people.

Unwise intercessors are disposed to promote their ministry or spiritual insights above people. Inclined to think of themselves more highly than they ought to think, contrary to Romans 12:3, people of prayer tend to congregate only with other intercessors who *validate* them, rather than stick with spiritual Christians who offer spiritual accountability. If there are no mature intercessors among them they can easily fall victim to cliques and cliches.

Even with the incredible strengths warfare intercessors offer, these spiritual activists can be some of the quickest members to get out of line. Pastors must learn to love and critique them, without being critical.

We have noticed pastors commonly make one of two mistakes concerning their intercessors. They either have an inflated view of intercessors, or a deflated view of them. Both views are unfair. Although intercessors can appear spiritually impressive and even a bit intimidating at times, a wise pastor will look at his intercessors' lives and get God's evaluation of their growth and development.

Like every other member of your church, each intercessor is at a different level of spiritual growth. As with any gift and calling, even a new believer can be an intercessor. So the fact that they are warlike, passionate or anointed is not necessarily indicative of maturity in Christ.

Pastor, as their spiritual leader, get to know your intercessors. Love and encourage them. Disciple them. Hold them accountable. Affirm them. Help release these Christians into their destiny in God. Provide a safe learning environment for them. All the while, pray that your heart and theirs will be knit together in love.

In the next chapter we'll outline what we feel pastors need from their intercessors.

CHAPTER SEVEN

What Intercessors Need From Their Pastors

Have you ever heard the story of Phocas, the fourth century Gardener Saint of Asia Minor?

Phocas lived in a little cottage outside the city gate of Sinope, Italy. Weary, hungry travelers passed the door of his cottage almost all hours of the day and night. By the holy ingenuity of love he stopped as many of them as possible to offer them rest, friendly conversation and a bit of food from his well-tended garden—in Jesus' name.

Suddenly one day life changed for Phocas. Orders went out from the Roman Emperor Diocletian that all Christians were to be put out of business. The soldiers, under orders to find the man named Phocas and put him to death, were about to enter the city one hot afternoon when they passed in front of the old man's cottage and garden. In his innocence he treated them as though they were his warmest friends, begging them to stay awhile and rest themselves. They consented. Phocas' hospitality was so warm and gracious that when he invited them to stay the night and go on their way refreshed the next day, they agreed.

"And what is your business?" Asked Phocas, unsuspectingly.

The soldiers then told him that they would answer his question if he would keep it a secret. It was obvious to them by now that he was a man to be trusted. The men told Phocas that they were Roman persecutors searching for a Christian man named "Phocas."

"Please sir, if you know Phocas, would you be so good as to help us identify him. After all, he is a dangerous follower of this Jesus about whom the Christians talk, and he must be executed immediately."

"I know him well," replied Phocas, quietly. "In fact, he is quite near. Let's attend to it in the morning."

His guests having retired, Phocas sat thinking. Escape? That would be easy. He only had to leave under cover of darkness. At daybreak he could be at least twenty miles away. He knew fellow Christians who would hide him. When the persecution had passed, he could reappear and once again cultivate his garden.

The decision to flee to safety or to stay unto death was apparently made without struggle or delay. Phocas went out into his garden and began digging in the darkness. There wasn't any earthly thing he loved more than this little plot of ground—the odor of the humus, the feel of the soil, the miracle of fertility. What were his thoughts as he continued digging?

There was still time to run away. But Jesus didn't run from his Gethsemane or his Calvary. Or, perhaps he thought of his Christian friends to whom he might run for asylum. Would their hiding him endanger them? As for his executioners who were now soundly sleeping in his cottage, they were, after all, only men who were carrying out orders. If they failed to find their man, the soldier's own lives would most likely be taken.

Deeper and deeper Phocas dug. Before dawn he was done. There it was—his own grave.

Morning came, and with it the waking of the assassins. "I am Phocas," he admitted calmly. A Christian bishop who recorded this story for posterity said that the men stood "motionless" in astonishment. They couldn't believe it! And when they did believe it, they obviously were reluctant to execute without mercy a man who had shown them nothing but mercy.

It was the persuasion of Phocas himself that overcame their reluctance. They had a duty to perform. He knew it. He was not bitter at them. Besides, he assured them he had no fear of death. Toward them he bore nothing but the love of Christ.

Moments later it was all over. The sword had done its work. And the body of Phocas, Christ's love-mastered man, lay dead in the garden he had loved so dearly.

Like Phocas, pastors have the unique privilege of tending the garden of God. They spend many long hours in study and prayer, often showing mercy when judgment is deserved. And most pastors willingly lay down their lives for the good of others. You can contribute to a mighty Kingdom harvest pastor, if you will earnestly seek to meet the needs of your intercessors. Let's look at a few.

1. They need to be loved.

In the story of Phocas, we learn the power of love. We are also confronted with the lack of love that exists in so many of our hearts.

Praying people, like everyone, need godly *affection*. Love, encourage and express your appreciation to your intercessors. Provide a safe place for them to learn and to risk in your church. When they mess up, encourage them to try again. Remind intercessors that no one is perfect.

2. They need a true ministry partnership.

As pastors understand the importance of intercession and the interdependence between pastor and intercessor, they are beginning to apply the principles of team building.

At times it can feel as if intercessors and pastors are working at odds with each other. In fact, they are working at opposite ends of the same spectrum. Their assignments and perspectives are different. But both are working to extend the

Kingdom of God. There are times when we bring our intercessors to alert. There are times when they alert us.

3. They need a clear understanding of your ministry vision.

"Then the LORD answered me and said: 'Write the vision and make it plain on tablets, that he may run who reads it'" (Habakkuk 2:2).

Intercessors are people of vision. They are set on "go." If they don't know the pastor's vision for the church, they can get out of sync. Anyone can cast a vision to intercessors. Many times the intercessor, who is called of God to support the vision of the pastor, has little or no idea what the pastor's vision might be. They can become frustrated in their prayer ministry and either drop out or flake out by excesses. Pastor, write down your vision and make it plain to the intercessors who have chosen to partner with you.

Don't be threatened by intercessors. Get them on board with your vision for the church. You might be surprised to find that the intercessors are receiving key revelation to help fulfill your personal and ministry goals. Hearing from them might even convince you that your vision is too small. Some pastors enlist the aid of their intercessors to capture, confirm and crystallize the Lord's vision for their church. After all, there is safety in a multitude of counselors (see Proverbs 24:6).

4. They need a good communication system.

Intercessors thrive on communication. They use the information for "prayer fuel." When leadership fails to communicate their needs for prayer, intercessors interpret that to mean that they are considered unnecessary. We have sought, even with our busy traveling schedule, to write a letter every couple of months sharing our prayer requests and praise reports. Included is a travel schedule for the intercessors who love to intercede in a more structured, patterned way.

Occasional fellowships are needed. Some pastors schedule breakfasts and banquets for their intercessors. These functions allow the intercessors to develop meaningful ministry relationships among themselves as well as with church leadership. Don't overlook the opportunity of praying for each other.

Meaningful ministry partnership is dependent upon two-way communication. Don't be afraid to ask the intercessors what they think God is saying for the church, city or nation. Get their feedback and show gratitude when they risk sharing their insights. We are amazed at how many intercessors from other churches call us with questions and concerns. Our first question is, "What does your pastor say?" Sadly, too often they explain that their pastor is either inaccessible, or unwilling to partner with them.

Intercessors also need to feel *appreciated* by their pastors. Intercession is largely done in secret. To them it is an act of loving obedience to God—not to the instructions of man. We all agree that our primary job as pastors is to see what the Father is doing and join him. (See John 5:19.) Listen to this, *"But you, when you pray, go into your room, and when you have shut your door, pray to your Father who is in the secret place; and your Father who sees in secret will reward you openly"* (Matthew 6:6, NKJV). This verse says that the Father acknowledges the intercessor and rewards them openly. That being the case, so should we.

Prayer warriors need appropriate access to you. The keyword here is *appropriate*. You will have to teach them how and when that is to be done. Pastors and intercessors of differing genders must exercise caution when meeting together. I

(Eddie) always schedule these appointments when the secretarial staff is in the office. In fact, I always leave my office door ajar. Beyond that, I always share with Alice the issues I am discussing with female intercessors. Obviously, the best approach would be to have another female in the room. But that is not always possible. The key point we are making is—exercise discernment.

You will need to teach your staff and the other leaders in your church how to integrate prayer and the prayer ministers (intercessors) of your church, in the planning of their programs and activities.

They also need to be *visible in the congregation*. Godly, praying people don't desire undue attention that would provoke them to pride, or others to jealousy. However, occasional rightful honor as you would give faithful teachers, home group pastors, deacons and musicians *is* in order. These "ministers of prayer" need to be heard and respected, not ignored or suppressed. The level of visibility and the respect you publicly show your intercessors communicates to the rest of your congregation the value you place on prayer.

Tell the intercessors when they are right. Let them know that they are a valued part of your ministry. Honor them without showing partiality. You can build their confidence without building their pride.

5. They need spiritual accountability.

There are three pastors in Houston that I (Eddie) relate to as *my pastors*. Technically, they are not my pastors. However, practically, they are. I routinely seek their counsel and submit to them in accountability. It's not that they are accountable *for me*. It's that I choose to be accountable *to them*. There is a great sense of security knowing they are there.

I encourage you to develop relationships of accountability with pastors who you respect, who know you well enough to speak into your life. Your intercessors need that same sense of spiritual security. You should provide them with a place of safety where there is freedom to fail. Perhaps your warfare intercessors need it most. They need the freedom to risk what they feel God may be saying, knowing that you can judge their word, without judging them. After all, hearing God's voice is difficult. Clarity in hearing and wisdom in understanding come only with maturity.

In his book, *Pastors of Promise*, pastor/author Jack Hayford explains,

"In some of the life stories I relate, I will often say, 'The Lord spoke to me.' This terminology can be sorely misunderstood, so when I say 'God speaks,' I am making a specific statement predicated upon certain scriptural truths.

First, I certainly do not see myself as preferred above anyone, more as a candidate for new revelations. I believe, however, that God speaks to everyone—to every human being, both by general and specific revelation.

⋄ The starry *heavens* bear testimony to his eternal power and Godhead (see Psalms 19; Romans 1:20). Creation itself testifies to its Creator, which is the reason an internalized awe and 'sense of God' moves us when we gaze at the night sky, ponder the relentless tides of the sea or look into a baby's eyes.

⋄ The *conscience* is an inner voice of God (see Romans 2:14,15). This secret point of inescapable awareness and accountability is present in one way or another in virtually every person. Conscience may be smothered and silenced—even seared or burned over—but it cannot be escaped.

◇ God speaks in the *Bible*, the conclusive written Word of God (see Romans 10:17). Here is the source of his clear and analyzable revelation, where propositional truth is synthesized and practical understanding made fully accessibly available.

◇ God has spoken in his only begotten Son, *Jesus* of Nazareth. The character, actions, miracles, teaching, life and death of Jesus are all expressions of God's living Word. He has spoken in Christ—and continues to speak through the testimony of Jesus, which you and I bear to others.

◇ God speaks to people in the *church assembly*, as the Holy Spirit prompts someone with a word from the Lord (see 1 Kings 19:12, 13; 1 Corinthians 14:1-5). Such subjective words must always remain in alignment with established principles of his timeless Word. The Spirit of prophecy never speaks to add anything to the Scriptures, but to apply the eternal Word of the Scriptures—practically, powerfully and vitally to us—at given points of needed understanding.

◇ He also speaks to us by the example of godly *relatives* whose influence marks so many, through their character and by prayer (2 Timothy 1:5).

By these means, then, humans experience direct messages from the almighty God, to whom we will all have to give account. So you can understand why I am not hesitant to say, 'God spoke to me.' Since he communicates so fully and freely with us, even *prior* to our new birth, it should not be surprising he *continues* to do so in even more personal ways once we become his children.

For my part, the 'voice' of the Lord comes in different ways. When describing it, at times, I feel virtually able to say, 'And I quote.' Yet at other times I am only referencing impressions, a sense of prompting, or a quickening of memory. As tens of thousands of believers do, I believe it is important for us to learn to hear and respond to such dealings of the Holy Spirit. I also yearn for the day and am hopeful we may find a time when arguments, reticence or critical rejection of such intimacy with God will be past."[1]

6. They need training.

Intercessors need continual instruction. Like the other members of the church, intercessors don't come fully grown. Intercession is not a measure of maturity, it is a focus of ministry. They need pastoral leadership.

Pastor, your intercessors need to know that you love them enough to give them godly direction and gentle correction when necessary. When it becomes necessary to confront and correct an intercessor, do so privately, personally, directly and most of all do it lovingly! Show honor by not broadcasting the intercessor's problem to your entire staff. The respect you show people of prayer will pay off down the road.

Don't ignore issues, or put off dealing with problems. If you fail to act, you will be forced to deal with them in the future at more inopportune times when the stakes are higher.

Your prayer warriors know they are *different*. As we have pointed out, the life of the intercessor is unusual. Many of them are misunderstood and tend toward feelings of insecurity, so pastoral reassurance helps. Just as miners who work underground must come above ground to see the result of their labor, intercessors who labor alone in their prayer closets are looking for evidence that their labor is not in vain. Pastoral affirmation can provide a lifelong relationship of love and encouragement as your intercessors learn to exercise the gifts that God has given them.

7. Intercessors also need to see integrity in their leaders.

They need to know beyond a doubt that their pastor is pursuing God with all his heart. They need to know that he values prayer. Pastor, your intercessors know that your greatest strength lies in your humility before God and man. Preaching prayer without practicing it will undermine your relationship.

How to Relate to Your Intercessors

1. Be transparent and humble. Pastor, if you are not an intercessor, tell them you aren't. At the same time, pray with them occasionally so they can see your commitment to prayer. Show your respect for their ministry as you seek respect for your own.

2. Don't play favorites or engage in clickish behavior with, or to the exclusion of your intercessors.

3. Do not belittle intercessors or subtly punish them for believing they've heard or are hearing something that may challenge you as a pastor.

4. God sometimes uses them to challenge us. Sure they will miss it at times. But our best position with our intercessors is to try and hear God through them —even if the message is not delivered perfectly.

5. Do not overlook adequate logistical support, whether that is office administrators, or church building accessibility. Designate funds in your budget to provide adequate supplies, maps, tapes, resources, training and staff that will encourage your intercessors. This kind of action will prove you have their best interest at heart.

CHAPTER EIGHT

What Pastors Need
From Their Intercessors

Prayer is the pastor's primary protection against spiritual attack. Fervent, effective, focused prayer is his greatest asset. Simply put, every pastor needs a shield of prayer surrounding his life, his family and ministry. Pastors and all Christian leaders need intercessors. The need to partner with intercessors and surrender the time and energy necessary to build an effective prayer shield are keys for successful ministry.

An Intercessor's Warning

"If in doubt—don't," wrote Robin White, one of our personal intercessors in an email message to me (Eddie).

"Incredible!" I said aloud even though no one else was in the room. For about a week I had been encouraged by a friend to call a particular pastor and inquire about a church issue. Yet there was a reservation in my heart. If you know me at all, you know I am rarely shy about anything!

Shrugging off what I thought was senseless, unreasonable doubt, I picked up the phone to call the pastor. But before placing the call, I decided to check my email. Voila! There it was—my answer! Robin's email said, "If in doubt—don't." So, I didn't. Later that day I learned how tragic that call would have been had it been made.

I called Robin later to thank her for warning me. Of course, she never knew the specifics, but she was appreciative and encouraged that her intercession had made a difference.

For more than ten years we have had over fifty personal intercessors that make up our prayer shield. They pray for us, our family and for our ministry. Our prayer shield often hears from God regarding the things with which we are involved. What they hear God say becomes "fuel" for their intercession. Sometimes they report to us what they've heard.

◇ Our intercessors are *like family*. They are our brothers and sisters in Christ. As you know, spiritual family can in some ways be as meaningful as natural family.

◇ Our intercessors are *our friends*. We genuinely love them and enjoy their fellowship. God has promised that those who receive a prophet will also receive a prophet's reward. (See Matthew 10:41.) We fully expect that any reward we will receive as ministers will be accounted to those who have stood beside us, those who have upheld our hands in prayer and have been our partner in ministry. Only God knows how much of our spiritual success will result from their labor of love in the prayer closet!

The mistake that most leaders make when forming a prayer shield, is soliciting people to serve as their intercessors.

Pastor, if you don't have a prayer shield we strongly urge you to ask God for one. The mistake that most leaders make when forming a prayer shield, is soliciting people to serve as their intercessors. There are at least three reasons we feel that is unwise.

First, few mature intercessors will take requests for long-term assignments. They know that their long-term assignments come from the Lord. They know the weight of such a responsibility and will hesitate to make such a commitment without a sure word from God and the promise of his grace to complete it.

Second, some immature intercessors will be flattered that you've asked and will jump at a chance to have "inside access" to leadership. They will most often accept the invitation only to become weary after a season, and drop out from a sense of guilt.

Finally, those who God often raises up are people you would never have selected. But if they are to be effective and remain, they need to be God-called, not man-chosen.

We suggest that if you do not have a prayer shield that you ask the Father for intercessors (see Matthew 9:37-38). God will hear and answer your prayer. Once you have asked, then begin to listen closely to what people say to you. You will begin to hear statements like, "Pastor, the Lord has really had me praying for you lately." Or, "Pastor, I've really had you on my heart this week." When you hear those comments you should immediately ask, "Do you feel that God is calling you to intercede for me?" As they acknowledge and accept God's call, then begin communicating your needs to them. You prayed for intercessors, so God called and commissioned them! Then he revealed them to you. You didn't recruit them in the usual sense of the word. These are the best kind of prayer warriors to have. If you would like to learn more about how to find your intercessors, we suggest C. Peter Wagner's book *Prayer Shield* published by Regal Books.

1. Your pastor needs his privacy.

Intercessor, prayer is your passion and pursuit. Your pastor, like most pastors, may not be an intercessor. It is just one of many ministry items (missions, teaching, counseling, evangelism and administration) that he must address.

Because of this, you should be sensitive to his personality, spiritual gifts, ministry focus and to the type of ministry partnership he offers you as an intercessor.

Sometimes intercessors find it hard to accept the fact that they may not be able to experience a close personal friendship with the senior pastor. A pastor and his wife should enjoy the freedom to select their own circle of friends. "Partnership" and "communication" don't necessarily mean social closeness. These words describe a function for a purpose.

There may be rare instances when "all the best" of relationships come together. But because of the nature of friendships, that too may pass or change. Human relationships are ever-changing and at best temporary. Try to avoid imposing eternal dynamics on relationships. Don't look to man for those things that only God can provide.

Because of time restraints or the sheer size of their congregation, some pastors assign pastoral staff to interface with their intercessors on a routine day-to-day basis. This staff member needs to be well-acquainted with intercessors and intercession. They should be sensitive to the intercessors' unique needs. The recognized prayer leader should, as a rule, have access to the senior pastor.

2. Pastors need your understanding as well as your prayer.

Having been reared in a pastor's home. I (Eddie) am convinced that the average church member has no idea the level of pressure that rests on the shoulders of pastors.

◇ Pastors are on-call 24-hours a day, seven days a week. Even policemen and firemen have their days off. Church member emergencies can always interrupt a pastor's day off, or even his family vacation.

◇ Most of us work for a boss. Of course it isn't true, but the average church member feels as though his pastor works for him. He thinks, "If he doesn't measure up, we'll fire him and hire us a pastor who does." Imagine yourself having 300-400 bosses!

◇ The visibility of leadership means that your pastor "lives in a glass house." When I (Eddie) was in elementary school, there was a time when the ladies' Sunday school class met in our house, the parsonage next door to the country church that my father pastored. In many ways, a pastor and his family are constantly "on trial." What they do, what they say, what they wear and where they go is always being scrutinized.

All of us, pastors and laity, were born on a battlefield. From our first breath to our last, we are living amidst an ancient war between cosmic forces, God and Satan. Christian ministry is in reality a battle for worshipers, for souls and ultimately for the nations of the earth. Satan doesn't shoot blanks. The dangers and the casualties are real (John 10:10).

◇ Spiritual leaders are like commissioned officers in God's army. A pastor may as well have a target painted on his back on which Satan's guns are trained. We are constantly hearing of pastors who have lost their health to sickness and disease, lost their mental or emotional balance due to stress and overwork, lost their spiritual vitality (Titus 1:7-9), or have lost their faith and have fallen out of the ministry by falling into sin. Satan prefers to target your pastor and his family because he knows that one of the best ways to defeat the church is to shame its leaders.

◇ Your pastor's family is also in the cross hairs of the devil's sight. Satan loves to inflict pain on a pastor by causing his wife to suffer accident, illness, or disease. He targets ministers' marriages and takes pot shots at their children. A pastor's child is a favorite "bull's-eye" for the devil. Young and easily deceived, they are often unfairly held to a higher standard than their peers simply because of who their father is. Many eyes are on them. And Satan knows that ministry anointing tends to increase generationally. Therefore the next generation can cause him to suffer even greater losses.

◇ True pastoral ministry is supernatural. No man can do it, regardless of how gifted or talented he is. Satan produces distractions, causes fruitlessness and stirs up divisions. He will do all he can to drum your pastor out of the ministry. Many pastors today are close to "drop out" or "burn out." And they know that they will be personally judged more strictly than others! (See James 3:1.) So the stakes are high!

◇ A pastor's faithfulness influences many others. When he falls, the cause of Christ is besmirched and many are wounded.

◇ The pastor carries great responsibility. He has been entrusted with God's work. Every time he makes a decision he can rest assured that part of the church will agree with it and another part will oppose it. He continually copes with the questions, "Did I handle that right?" Or, "Did I make the right decision?" Others are following his instruction and example. (See Matthew 15:14.) Pastor, we encourage you not to sweat the politics. God is quite able and willing to vindicate.

◇ Leadership carries enormous demands and extraordinary pressures. The pressures of ministry often require solutions that only intercession can provide.

The Institute of Church Growth at Fuller Seminary in Pasadena, California conducted a survey of pastors in 1991. The findings showed:

90% of pastors work more than 46 hours a week.

80% believe that pastoral ministry has affected their families negatively.

33% said that ministry is an outright hazard to their family.

75% reported a significant personal stress-

---

related crisis at least once in their ministry.

50% felt unable to meet the needs of their
job.

90% felt they were inadequately trained to
cope with ministry demands.

70% say they have lower self-esteem now than
when they started out.

40% reported a serious conflict with a church
member at least once a month.

70% do not have someone they consider a
close friend.

3. Your pastor needs your love.

Pastors often suffer the pain of shattered friendships. Many
are sheep-bitten, lonely, wounded or depressed from a constant barrage of criticism. Some even lose their lives due to
the crushing weight of ministry.

We have learned over the years that few people can
love a pastor like an intercessor. We think its because pastors
and intercessors, in one sense, have so much in common.

◇ Like pastors, intercessors have a pastoral heart. Why
else would they spend so much time "giving away their lives in
the prayer closet" for others?

◇ Intercessors, like pastors, know they are called into
the ministry they perform. Their prayer closet is as much a
calling as his pulpit!

◇ Both pastors and intercessors are visionaries.

These and other similarities cause intercessors to be
particularly capable of loving leadership. The true gift of
heaven sent intercession is expressed by love.

Love's Prerogative

Love ever gives--
Forgives--outlives--
And ever stands
With open hands.
And while it lives--
It gives
For this is love's prerogative--
To give--and give--and give.[1]

--John Oxenham

CHAPTER NINE

The Conclusion of History

"Most scholars agree that the total amount of human knowledge doubled once between 4,000 BC and the birth of Christ. Then from the birth of Christ to 1750, it doubled again. From 1750 to 1900, it doubled again. From 1900 to 1950, it doubled again. Notice how the time frames get shorter and shorter from 4,000 years to 1,700 years, to 150 years, to 50 years. Then from 1950 to 1960, it doubled again, and now, in this generation, the rate has become exponential. The prominent belief now is that the rate of doubling is less than two years.

Think about that. Every two years, the sum total of all our human knowledge doubles! Never before in history has the near future seemed so intimidating." [1]

God's wisdom is the antidote
to exploding knowledge.
God's power is the antidote
to satanic activity.
And prayer is the doorway to both!
(See James 1:5; Luke 24:49.)

Restoring His Church, Preparing His Bride

We are living in exciting times as Daniel 12:4 states, *"knowledge shall increase."* Many believe we are living in the days preceding the second coming of the Lord. There is no doubt that God is pouring out his Spirit around the world. (See Joel 2:28.) Pastors and intercessors need to prepare for this great outpouring. The church is moving from adolescence to adulthood, thereby releasing the operation of the officers mentioned in Ephesians 4:11.

On a short-term mission trip in Riga, Latvia in 1990, I (Eddie) was interceding for the church. "Lord Jesus," I said, "Your church is a mess. Your bride is sick. She is paranoid and schizophrenic. She fights herself and bites herself. She suffers from Alzheimer's disease. She forgets who she is, to whom she is married, where her home is, and what she is suppose to be doing while she's here on Earth."

The Lord replied, "Eddie, you are right. My bride is sick. But just like any other husband with a sickly wife, I love her as she is. And Eddie, until you *love my bride like I love her, you don't love me.*"

That encounter changed my life. Most of us sense that Christ is coming for his bride very soon. However, Christ will not come for a sickly wife. Scripture tells us that " *. . . Christ loved the church and gave himself up for her to make her holy, cleansing her by the washing with water through the word, and to present her to himself as a radiant church, without stain or wrinkle or any other blemish, but holy and blameless"* (Ephesians 5:25-27 NIV).

Like all brides, she too will make herself ready. *"Let us rejoice and be glad and give him glory! For the wedding of the Lamb has come, and* his *bride has made herself ready. Fine linen, bright and clean, was given her to wear"* (Fine linen represents the righteous acts of the saints) (Revelation 19:7-8 NIV). Jesus Christ is coming for a prepared and faithful bride.

The Last Great Battle

As history records, there is always a great harvest of souls when the church experiences revival. The harvest is the ultimate point of a spiritual awakening. In this last battle, the church will rise and challenge Satan for the billions of lost souls yet standing in the valley of decision. Part of our coming into adulthood is our accepting the responsibility for lost humanity and a willingness to do something about it.

What are some of the recent signs of this happening?
⬦ Restoring the challenge of the Great Commission
⬦ Restoring praise and worship
⬦ Restoring fervent prayer and fasting
⬦ Restoring the role of the prophet
⬦ Restoring the role of the apostle

In the 1980s we saw the church ignited with the idea of completing the Great Commission. Every major Christian denomination set goals of doing so by the year 2000. World evangelization for example, was the focus of the *AD2000 & Beyond Movement.* The result has been a dramatic increase in revival and spiritual awakening around the world. In fact, the decade of the '90s we saw world evangelism almost triple!

In the late 1980s we also watched as a revival of praise and worship swept the globe. By the early '90s all the nations on earth were singing the same praise and worship songs. Even the streets were filled with praise during the global marches for Jesus.

In the '90s God began restoring prayer and fasting to the church. Churches across America have built prayer rooms, hired staff to pastor prayer and now consider prayer as a vital ministry of the church. Fasting with prayer, even forty-day fasts, have become commonplace in today's Christian society.

In the early 1990s the Spirit of God fanned into flame the prophetic gifts. The church began to hear God as well as read about him. We now are beginning to understand and utilize the prophetic gifts God has given his people.

In the latter '90s the church became aware not only of the role of prophet, but of the role of apostle. The offices of apostle and prophet are foundational to the work of the church *"until we all reach unity in the faith and in the knowledge of the Son of God and become mature, attaining to the whole measure of the fullness of Christ."* (See Ephesians 4:11-13, 2:20-22.) Yes, God is restoring biblical government in the church. When true biblical church government is reestablished, we will be in a better position to complain about civil government, and effectively challenge Satan's government.

Just as the Old Testament kings led Israel's armies into battle, the New Testament apostles (the pastors of the pastors, or city-elders) under the command of their Captain the Lord of Hosts, will soon lead the church into the last great battle against Satan's headquarters located in the second heaven. Satan and his hoards will be no match for a purified and unified church under the leadership of her Bridegroom the King of Glory! The gates shall not prevail against her. Fighting from her knees, Christ's bride will push back the darkness for a period during which perhaps billions will have an opportunity to be saved.

Isaiah gives us a window through which to see this last day church. *"I will give you the treasures of darkness, riches stored in secret places, so that you may know that I am the LORD, the God of Israel"* (Isaiah 45:3 NIV).

What Greater Things?

The church will soon be called to battle on higher levels than ever before. Literally, Jesus said, *"I tell you the truth, anyone who has faith in me will do what I have been doing. He will do even greater things than these, because I am going to the Father"* (John 14: 12).

The big question is, "What are the *greater works* of which Jesus spoke, and when will the church do them?"

For 2000 years the church has proclaimed the Gospel, delivered the captives, healed the sick and raised the dead. Church history records that every generation since Christ's ascension has had the testimony of these expressions of the Gospel's power. Paul announces, *"My message and my preaching were not with wise and persuasive words, but with a demonstration of the Spirit's . . ."* (1 Corinthians 2:4 NIV).

God, who is no respecter of persons, has chosen that men and women of every generation rest their faith on more than mere words. He has produced signs, wonders and demonstrations of power through his church. The church has done the works of Jesus.

To understand the *greater* works, we must first examine the *works* Jesus did. The disciples knew that Jesus' works were the miracles that he performed and taught them to perform. They were proclaiming the Gospel, healing the sick, casting out demons and raising the dead. These could be characterized as works of light, liberty and life.

If his works were works of light, liberty and life, then it stands to reason that the *greater works* of which he spoke would be also.

Further, the word translated "greater" in this passage is most frequently used in Scripture in a *qualitative* sense rather than a *quantitative* sense. Qualitative suggests the quality of something, quantitative suggests an amount. Many have believed that Jesus was saying that because there are more of us, we would do more works than he did (amount). But we should remember that even before Jesus died, his disciples were already doing his works. So the fact that there were more of the disciples, and only one Jesus, didn't qualify as greater works, just more of the same works.

Besides, the healing of hundreds of blind eyes is not qualitatively different than the healing of one blind eye. It is only quantitatively different. It is the same miracle done many times.

It's like the difference between one pea and a plate of peas. The plate contains more peas, not necessarily greater peas. That is quantitative. However, a single four-pound pea is qualitatively different!

That's what Jesus was saying. We would do similar, but qualitatively greater works that express light, liberty and life! But what could these greater works be?

Of all the works that Jesus did, there is one area of ministry that the Heavenly Father never released to Jesus. Scripture does not suggest that Jesus ever directly or intentionally confronted territorial principalities, powers and rulers of the darkness. (See Ephesians 3:10, 6:12.)

He confronted, silenced and expulsed common, everyday, run-of-the-mill demons that reside in people. In the wilderness temptation Jesus also directly confronted and confounded Satan. However, Jesus never gave specific attention to what many theologians call *the second heaven* realm of the Ephesians 6:12 majesties.

Let's not overlook the mystery mentioned in Ephesians 3:9-10. Paul writes that the Father gave the church the assignment of revealing the secrets of God that have been hidden since the beginning of time. Directly and clearly, verse 10 states the purpose. *"His* (God's) *intent that now, through the church, the manifold wisdom of God should be made known to the rulers and authorities in the heavenly realms."*

What was God's intention?

1. Reveal salvation to both Greek and Hebrew.

2. Authorize them as ambassadors to do his work.

3. Drive out evil spirits and heal sicknesses and disease.

4. Manifest the delegated power of the church to the principalities and powers in heavenly realms.

Proof is in the Word

Jesus neither belittled nor ridiculed Satan. In fact, he conversed with him in the wilderness using only the Word of God to answer. However, his approach with the ground-level demon was totally different. He confronted, silenced and expulsed them. This teaches us that there are different ways of dealing with the different levels of the enemy's forces.

Jesus only did and said what the Father was doing and saying. It is clear from Scripture that although Jesus told Satan to "be gone" at the end of his wilderness test (see Matthew 4:10), the Father neither directed Jesus to bind Satan nor to confront Satan's territorial hierarchy. (See John 5:19.)

Example: In Mark 4:35-41 we read where Jesus invited the disciples to cross the Sea of Galilee one evening. While they were sailing, a very strong wind came and angry waves began splashing over the sides of the boat. It was filling with water.

Jesus was asleep in the back of the boat during the storm. His friends woke him and said, "Teacher, do you care about us? We will drown!"

Jesus stood up and commanded the wind and the waves to stop. He said, "Quiet! Be still!" The wind stopped and the lake became calm.

Next Jesus said to them, "Why are you so fearful. Where's your faith?"

The followers, very much afraid, asked each other, "What kind of man is this? Even the wind and the waves obey him!"

It is likely that the storm Jesus experienced while he was crossing the Sea of Galilee on his way to Gadara was the result of his crossing into another *spiritual territory*. (See Mark Chapter 5.) The Gadarene demoniac was likely the *human host* to the territorial spirit or spirits of that region. Why? For three reasons:

First, the demonic power at work in the man of Gadara was on a greater level than typical demonization. Even chains could not hold this man (see Mark 5:3-5).

Second, the spirits that were cast out of the demoniac specifically asked not to be sent out of the territory. (See Mark 5:10.) Amazingly Jesus conceded and didn't send them out of the territory! Why? Because to have done so, would have been a direct provocation of the territorial powers. The Father had not released that assignment to Jesus. He would have been picking a premature fight. (See John 5:30, 15:5.)

Third, the response of the city once the Gadarene was freed was completely out of balance. A city that was once fearful of the demonized man was now fearful of Jesus and demanded that he leave. (See Matthew 8:33-34.) Obviously, the city was under the demonic spell of these ruling spirits.

Is Satan Territorial?

There is a debate in the church today about whether or not Satan is territorial. That's really the wrong question. Sheer logic demands that we start the debate at the beginning. The real question is, "Is God territorial?" Indeed he is!

⬥ He not only created, he also measured the earth. (See Isaiah 40:12; Habakkuk 3:6.)

⬥ He assigned "the Promised Land" to Israel and assigned a specific territory to each tribe. (See Deuteronomy 32:8.)

Jehovah is territorial. He assigns his servants to specific, identifiable territories. The Apostle Paul knew his God-given territorial assignment and was certain that he had not crossed into another man's spiritual territory. (See 2 Corinthians 10:13-16.)

You too have a territory. Have you identified it? Your territory is a specific area of spiritual influence. It is greater than any physical influence you may possess. Chuck Pierce and Becky Sytsema, in their book *Possessing Your Inheritance* say it this way: "When God is ready to make covenant with you over your portion, he already has the plan for how you can inherit it."[3] Each one of us will give account to God for the stewardship of our spiritual territorial assignment. As we possibly are living in the conclusion of history, let's be diligent to identify, claim and take our territory.

Yes, God is territorial. And Satan has said in his heart, *"I will be like the Most High"* (Isaiah 14:14).

Besides, unlike God, Satan is not omnipresent. In order to carry out his assignments and to accomplish his plan, Satan is of necessity territorial. Sadly, Satan successfully carries out his ancient territorial strategy as theologians sit idly by arguing over him and his purposes. Study the following report of Satan's strategy.

> *12 "When the Lord has finished all his work against Mount Zion and Jerusalem, he will say, 'I will punish the king of Assyria for the willful pride of his heart and the haughty look in his eyes.'*
>
> *13 For he says: 'By the strength of my hand I have done this, and by my wisdom, because I have understanding. I removed the boundaries of nations, I plundered their treasures; like a mighty one I subdued their kings.*
>
> *14 As one reaches into a nest, so my hand reached for the wealth of the nations; as men gather abandoned eggs, so I gathered all the countries; not one flapped a wing, or opened its mouth to chirp'"*
> (Isaiah 10:12-14).

◇ Satan is filled with pride.
◇ He is an ancient deity with strength in his hand and manifests wisdom and understanding.

⬧ He has successfully removed the spiritual boundaries of the nations.

⬧ He has plundered their treasures (the souls of men, women, boys and girls.)

⬧ He has subdued their kings (by deceiving religious, political and social leaders.)

⬧ He has gathered the wealth (the value) of the nations as a man would gather eggs.

⬧ All the while, the church has not *"flapped a wing, or opened its mouth to chirp."* We have yet to contend with him!

Brother Andrew relates the following story about the importance of our setting a standard in a lost and dying world.

> "A couple of years ago at an Open Doors prayer conference, an old friend was talking to me over dinner about how hard it is to present the Gospel in a world controlled by evil powers. 'I know we must become more confrontational and aggressive,' he said. 'But how can we manage to battle the enemy in a hostile world and still represent nothing but the love of Christ?'"
>
> "I answered him by telling a story about the time Corrie ten Boom and I were in a meeting in Holland in which the group was discussing the same problem. Somehow we had gotten off on a tangent into a conversation about thermostats for heating and cooling systems. It was not such a strange tangent, really, when you consider that Corrie was fascinated by everything technical. She was, as you remember, a watchmaker by trade, and

she loved anything that moved — from watches to people, and everything in between."

"As it happened, everyone in the room that day seemed to know something about thermostats, and Corrie was bent on understanding how they worked. Once we satisfied her curiosity, Corrie said, 'Tell me, what's the difference between a thermostat and a thermometer?'"

"Several more minutes of explanation followed, until Corrie's eyes lit up with understanding and she began to nod."

"'Yes, I see,' she said. 'A thermometer only indicates what the temperature is. But a thermostat changes the temperature.' Then she practically jumped out of her chair. 'Andrew!' She exclaimed. 'That's the answer to our problem! We've got to be thermostats — not thermometers!'"

"Thermostats exist to change the situation. They don't merely register that it's too cold or too hot; they respond to our touch and actually alter the environment. In my office in the wintertime I can hear a little click in the thermostat when it goes on, and if I'm watching for it I can even see a little spark fly to make the connection. Then the central boiler swings into action and — boom — something changes. The whole mechanism of my heating system will fight the cold because I made a decision. I decided how warm it should be in my office, and the thermostat responded by changing the temperature."

> "This is exactly what we must do as Christians. We must understand that we were not created to be mere thermometers for the world, shaking our heads or clucking our tongues over how hot or cold it's getting. We were created to respond to the Holy Spirit's touch by clicking on, firing up our boilers, and causing change. God has placed in our hands the power and authority to do that."[2]

Pastors and intercessors alike are to be "thermostats" continually working to improve the spiritual climate of our society! Not lukewarm, not cold, not complacent, but on fire for God. Let's fervently contend with the devil.

Hell's Gates and Treasures

We will see Christ's mature bride arrayed in purity, stand in unity, and declare with authority, "No more!"

Paul told us the assignment that the purified, unified church, clothed with the armor of God, would have concerning Satan and the second heaven. He said, *"Put on the full armor of God so you can take your stand against the devil's schemes"* (Ephesians 6:11). If there's no battle, who needs armor?

The devil's *schemes* are plotted at hell's headquarters, not among common, everyday, earthbound demons (satanic foot soldiers). *"Our struggle* (on the other hand) *is . . . against the rulers, against the authorities, against the powers of this dark world and against the spiritual forces of evil in the heavenly realms"* (Ephesians 6: 12).

So Paul identifies the church's struggle today. We confront and deal with common demons from time to time. But they are small stuff, like gnats along the way.

Pastor, it is time for you to equip yourself in the area of deliverance. For why would the Father assign to you and the church you lead with binding and defeating territorial or regional spirits if you are unprepared or afraid to cast a demon out of an individual? Let's prepare for the greater works that have been promised the church.

Intercessor, the Lord can't empower you with prayer authority over territorial spirits until you are faithful to pray for your pastor, your church, or your city. You need to learn how to help others receive freedom from demons as well. We have a tape series (audio and video) on deliverance called *Delivering the Captives.* It may be helpful.

The Lord Jesus has ultimately called the mature church to a *qualitatively* higher assignment. She has been called to confront hell's *rulers and authorities* that sit and scheme at hell's gates. Assaulting hell's gates and the rulers seated there is an assignment God is placing on the church. Just as Jesus prophesied, it is a greater earthly work that the Father has reserved for the bride of Christ. Jesus himself said, *". . . and the gates of Hades will not prevail against it* (the church)" (Matthew 16:18).

Yes, we are the generation who will see the church, Christ's mature bride, arrayed in purity, stand in unity and declare with authority to those ancient evil princes, "No more!" We are seeing this happen in nation after nation around the world. As it does, a massive spiritual harvest occurs.

The Ground War versus the Air War

The entire world impatiently held its breath waiting for the U.S.-led allied ground forces to assault Iraqi military positions during Desert Storm. It seemed to many of us that the ground war would never begin. General Schwartskoff explained that *the ground war could not begin until the air war was completed.*

As promised, once the air war was complete, the ground war began. And as hoped, the ground war was *a piece of cake.* The strength of Saddam's troops had been dissipated. His foot soldiers were disillusioned, tired and hungry. Their communications system was devastated. Hussein's soldiers surrendered on the spot.

In this spiritual war against the forces of darkness we see just the opposite. Prophetically gifted individuals can almost taste the air war. Warfare prayer intercessors are more than ready and willing. They've been revving up their engines for years. They can hardly wait until the Lord releases them against the gates of hell. Some are wondering, why not now? Others impatiently and presumptuously have decided to call their own shots. Like spiritual Rambos they are moving out, often without directives from our commander, Jesus Christ. They are conducting their spiritual sorties (air raids) only to see little change in their churches and cities. Many have suffered backlash and some have even died.

A few years ago we attended a spiritual warfare gathering in a southern city. After two hours of warfare singing the leader mounted the stage. "Everyone on your feet!" the leader yelled with the gusto of a drill-sergeant. And more than 700 people jumped to their feet obediently.

"Now everyone hold up your right hand!" came the order. The impassioned audience followed the leader. (Do you remember that game?)

"Now I want you to grab the tail of the Prince of Pride that rules over our city. Get a hold of Slue Foot's slimy old tail. Have you got it?" the leader queried.

The crowd thundered, "Yes!"

"Now on the count of three we're gonna pull the Prince of Pride down out of the heavenlies... are you ready? One, two, three... PULL!"

As we scanned the audience, we were shocked to see three small children (who had no idea what they were doing) standing beside an obese woman. Across the aisle from them stood a frail-looking man with a pack of Marlboro cigarettes in his shirt pocket. He was barely able to catch his next breath for the next cheer. Neither the woman nor the man had conquered their own bodies, yet they were being led to "assault ancient demonic deities."

King David first killed lions and bears, then he moved up to challenge giants. From there he graduated to taking cities and ultimately he conquered kingdoms. It was obvious that across the room there were few, if any, who should have been taunting territorial powers that night.

Some ask, "Why? Why should we wait?" The reason is simple. *The air war can't begin until the ground war is finished!* But what is the ground war? The ground war is the war within our own hearts

We cannot pull down strongholds with one hand that we support with our other.

and minds, and our relationships with each other. And we win this war face down in repentance and reconciliation. It's neither fun nor exciting. But we cannot pull down strongholds with one hand that we support with our other. It is our sin that supplies the strength for the satanic strongholds over our cities. Pride in the church strengthens the spiritual princes of pride that rule our cities. Our greatest need? Not to declare war on hell, but to declare war on our sin and disunity. If we don't clean up our act, repent of our pride, pursue integrity, establish a biblical foundation and some accountability in spiritual warfare, foolishness is going to derail the prayer movement!

We (God's church) are an out-of-shape army. We lack effective organization, communication, discipline, training, commitment and endurance. Too many pastors are concerned about "protecting the sheep," when in fact they are unwilling to challenge the sheep to leave their cream-puff, milk-toast self and be transformed into a lean, mean, spiritual fighting machine! Pastor, when it comes to equipping the saints, you are the drill sergeant that must challenge the church to get off "spiritual welfare" and into spiritual warfare!

God is gradually releasing some trained warfare intercessors into launching spiritual air raids. Other intercessors have been enlisted as guerilla warfare specialists, to fight against the entrenched pockets of darkness. But these assignments have at times come at a high price. Intercessors and pastors involved have counted the costs. Around the world seasoned men and women of prayer are laying down their very lives in the battle. This is the day of the martyr. (See Revelation 12:11.) This is not a game--this is real war with real casualties! So our advice is to understand what you are doing if you decide to pick a fight with the powers of darkness.

A Cry for the Nations!

During a Christian Broadcasting Network television news interview CBN reporter Chris Mitchell asked me (Eddie), "In your travel, what do you feel God is saying to the churches today about prayer?"

I said, "Alice and I hear an echo around the world in the various prayer conferences, retreats and seminars that we attend. Wherever we go, we invariably find ourselves in a prayer meeting. The last few years there is one prayer that is prayed with such passion and intensity that it stands out from all the rest. The church around the world is asking the Father for the nations. The unprecedented emphasis on praying for the nations and the unreached people groups is just one indication of that cry. That echo is a heart cry to the Father for the salvation of the nations."

In his book *Beyond Imagination*, Dick Eastman relates a breakthrough for Albania as a result of the efforts of the 10/40 Window campaign and other ministry organizations.

"As the plan was just getting underway, a team of thirty intercessors from Colorado Springs, led by Pastor Ted Haggard of New Life Church, traveled to Albania during the October 1993 'Pray through the Window' campaign. (It is estimated that more than twenty million believers participated in this month-long prayer campaign focused on the region referred to as the 10/40 Window, including about 249 teams of intercessors that actually visited the 10/40 Window countries during that month.) Strategic prayer was offered by Ted Haggard's team at various key sites, including at least one major 'high place' — a specific geographical demonic stronghold — in the mountains above Albania's capital of Tirana.

On returning to his congregation in Colorado Springs, Haggard not only mobilized his church for further prayer for Albania, but he enlisted their financial support to put feet to their prayers. New Life Church alone helped provide a Gospel message for every family in at least two thousand villages of Albania.

At this writing, the task of reaching every home in Albania is almost complete. Recent estimates indicated that as many as thirty villages are being reached in a single week. Many of those remaining are accessible only to evangelism teams traveling on donkeys or, in a few cases, by helicopter. More than 25 villages have been found so far that do not appear on any government maps, indicating that Christian workers are going to places even census takers have not visited.

One thing is certain: Cooperation is key to closure. It is also essential to speeding up the process." [4]

Our friend Ted Haggard, a mega-church pastor, is a friend of intercessors. He is a wonderful example of one who pastors, equips (even financially), and partners with intercessors. He is proof that what we are presenting in this book is not just theory, but consistently successful whenever this pastor-intercessor partnership is implemented.

The messianic prophecy, Psalm 2:8 says, *"Ask of me, and I shall give thee the heathen for thine inheritance, and the uttermost parts of the earth for thy possession."* KJV

We know that Jesus, the Great Intercessor, sits at the right hand of God the Father where he continually intercedes for us. (See Hebrews 7:25.) We also know that one day Jesus will ask the Father for the nations and that they will be given to him as an inheritance.

Prophecy Fulfilled

Christ is our head and we are his body. (See 1 Corinthians 12:12.) What the mouth, which is a member of the body speaks, is first conceived in the head. We are suggesting that the Psalm 2:8 prophecy is being fulfilled today. After 2000 years of church history, Christ in heaven is asking the Father for the nations as his inheritance. One proof is that it is also being spoken out of the mouth of his body here on earth. Another proof is that the nations really are coming to Christ in unprecedented numbers!

As intercessors and pastors (watchmen and gatekeepers), let's never forget this ultimate purpose for our partnership. After all:

⬦ We are joint-heirs with Christ (see Romans 8:17).

⬦ We are complete in Christ (see Colossians 2:9-10).

⬦ We are a kingdom of priests (see Revelation 1:6).

⬦ We are authorized and appointed (see Luke 10:19).

So, let's ask the Father today for the nations!

CHAPTER TEN

The Final Chapter

Pastors and intercessors, in a very real sense you are writing the final chapter. God is calling you to a new level of relationship...a true partnership. It will be forged with Christ's love in the furnace of trial. But this partnership is pregnant with the awesome power of Almighty God! It will require a new appreciation and respect for each other. Through it, we will discover a unique opportunity to more completely partner with Christ himself in his dual, yet singular role, as head of the church, ever-living to make intercession for us. Spurgeon, the great revivalist was preaching on the need of partnership when he said this:

> "A physician said: 'When I was a medical student I attended an operation where a great surgeon did the work. His assistant failed to come and he chose me to help him save that life. How proud I was to be chosen to help this great man!'" Spurgeon goes on to say: "I realized that God could save the world without me, but when he told me that I might help him I praised him for the honor and the privilege."[1]

We all agree with Spurgeon that God doesn't have to use us in his desire to save the world, but he has chosen us just the same! So we pastors and intercessors should catch the vision of partnership and begin sharing our burdens, our visions and our victories in one focused effort. With intercessory watchmen on our walls and pastoral gatekeepers at our gates working together, we can change our world! Let's do it!

NOTES

Chapter One
1. Max Lucado, *A Gentle Thunder* (Dallas, TX: Word Publishing, 1995), pg. 35.
2. Source: G. B .F. Hallock, *2500 Best Modern Illustrations* (New York and London: Harper & Brothers Publishers, 1935), pg. 242.

Chapter Two
None

Chapter Three
1. *Britannica Encyclopedia*, Grolier Addition CD Multimedia Edition, 1998.
2. Dutch Sheets, *Intercessory Prayer* (Ventura, CA: Regal Books, 1996) pg. 152.
3. Bob Moorehead, *Words Aptly Spoken* (Kirkland, WA: Overlake Christian Press, 1995), pp. 42-43.

Chapter Four
1. Jim Goll, *The Lost Art of Intercession* (Shippensburg, PA: Destiny Image, 1997) pg. 62.
2. Alice Smith, *Beyond the Veil* (Ventura, CA: Regal Publishing, 1997) pg. 33.
3. Eddie Smith, *Help! I'm Married to an Intercessor* (CA: Regal Publishing, 1998) pp. 23-24.
4. Oswald Chambers, *My Utmost for His Highest* (New York, NY: Dodd, Mead & Company, Inc., 1935) pg. 71.

Chapter Five
1. Sammy Tippit, Pray Then Preach, p. 17, *Spirit of Revival*, Dec 1999.
2. E.M. Bounds, *The Weapon of Prayer* (New Kensington, PA: Whitaker House, 1996), pg. 89.
3. Ted Haggard/Jack Hayford, *Loving Your City into the Kingdom* (Ventura, CA: Regal Books, 1997), pp. 160-162.

Chapter Six
1. Jonathan Benz, "Pastoring Intercessors," *Ministries Today*, Jan/Feb 2000, p.82.

Chapter Seven
1. Jack Hayford, *Pastors of Promise* (Ventura, CA: Regal Books, 1997), pp. 157-159.

Chapter Eight

1. Paul E. Holdcraft, *Cyclopedia of Bible Illustrations* (New York and Nashville: Abingdon-Cokesbury Press, 1957), pg. 174.

Chapter Nine

1. LaLonde, Peter & Paul, *2000AD Are You Ready?* (Nashville, TN: Thomas Nelson, 1997), pg. 23.

2. Brother Andrew, *And God Changed His Mind* (Old Tappan, NJ: Chosen Books, 1990), pp. 137-139.

3. Chuck Pierce & Becky Sytsema, *Possessing Your Ineritance* (Ventura, CA: Regal Books, 1999) pg. 113.

4. Dick Eastman, *Beyond Imagination* (Grand Rapids, MI: Chosen Books, 1997), pp. 278-279.

Chapter Ten

1. G. B .F. Hallock, *2500 Best Modern Illustrations* (New York and London: Harper & Brothers Publishers, 1935), pg. 386.

INDEX

C

Calvary 100
CBN 134
Cedar, Paul 1
Chambers, Oswald 65
chariots 33
charismatic 17, 81
Chief Cornerstone 34
Christian Broadcasting Network 134
Clarke, Ace and Joy 4, 19
cleanse the land 51
coexistence 20
collaboration 20
Colorado Springs, Colorado 77, 135
Columbus, Ohio 65
communication 19, 102, 103, 114
compassion 43
confirmation 90
conscience 106
consistent results 72
control 13, 15, 20, 94
cooperation 136
court 48
Covenant Centre International 88
covenant relationship 16
credibility 92
critical 56, 96
critical spirit 20

D

Dallas, Texas 13, 37, 68
Daniel 70
David 16, 50, 70
defiled land 49, 50, 56
deliverance 131
Delivering the Captives 131
denominationalism 16
dependence 28
Desert Storm 132

die to self 17, 42, 43
discern 18, 66, 87, 90
disunity 17
diversity 21, 22, 66
divisions 18
Doty, Sue 51

E

Eastman, Dick 77, 135
ecumenical movement 22
El Paso, Texas 65
Eli 71
Elijah 68, 70
evangelism 23, 121, 136
Every Home for Christ 77
excluded middle 87
Ezekiel 35, 36

F

failed trust 20, 40
faith 18, 41, 89, 123
faithful 96
faithfulness 16, 116
false prophets 68
family 112
fellowship 22
forgive 14, 15, 39
forgiveness 15, 43, 44, 45
forty-day fasts 121
friends 112
fuel 112
Fuller Seminary 116

G

Gadarene demoniac 125
Garden of Eden 74
Garden of Gethsemane 42
Gardener Saint of Asia Minor 99
gatekeepers 18, 19, 20, 30,
    31, 33, 45, 56, 57,
    64, 66, 137, 139

W

Appendix A
RESOURCE MINISTRIES

CHILDREN PRAYING

Children's Global Prayer Movement
Esther Network International
854 Conniston Road
W. Palm Beach, FL 33405
Phone: (561) 832-6490
Fax: (561) 832-8043
E-mail: lcci-eni@flinet.com

CITY STRATEGIES

Advancing Church Ministries
5300 North Park Place, N.E., Ste. 108
Cedar Rapids, IA 52402
Phone: (319) 373-9310
Fax: 319) 373-3012
E-mail: arrowacm@frangipane.org
Website: www.frangipane.org

Concerts of Prayer Greater New York
142-10 Sanford Ave.
Flushing, NY 11355
Phone: (718) 762-8232
Fax: (718) 762-8256
E-Mail: copiny@aol.com

Dawn Ministries
7899 Lexington Drive #200B
Colorado Springs, CO 80920
Phone: (719) 548-7460
Fax: (719) 548-7475
E-Mail: 71102.2745@compuserve.com

Mission America
901 E. 78th Street
Minneapolis, MN 55420
Phone: (612) 853-1762
Fax: (612) 853-1745
E-Mail: 74152.636@compuserve.com
Website: www.missionamerica.org

Concerts of Prayer International
P.O. Box 770
New Providence, NJ 07974
Phone: (908) 771-0146
Fax: (908) 665-4199
E-mail: copinj@aol.com
Website: www.copi.org

FASTING RESOURCES

Fasting for Spiritual Break Through (Book)
Elmer Town, Author
Liberty University
1971 University Boulevard
Lynchburg, VA 24502-2269
Phone: (804) 582-2169
Fax: (804) 582-2575
Website: www.elmertowns.com

Power Praying (Booklet)
Alice Smith, Author
U.S. Prayer Track
7710-T Cherry Park Dr. PMB 224
Houston, TX 77095
Phone: (713) 466-4009
Fax: (713) 466-5633
E-Mail: usprayertrack@cs.com
Website: www.usprayertrack.org

•**The 7 Basic Steps to Successful Fasting & Prayer**
•**The Transforming Power of Fasting & Prayer**
•**The Coming Revival**
•**Preparing For The Coming Revival**
Bill Bright, Author
New Life Publications
P.O. Box 593684
Orlando, FL 32859-3684
Phone: (800) 235-7255
Fax: (800) 514-7072
E-Mail: www.newlifepubs.com
Website: www.newlifepubs@ccci.org

LOCAL CHURCH PRAYER

Harvest Prayer Ministries
11991 East Davis Road
Brazil, IN 47834
Phone: (812) 443-5800
Fax: (812) 443-5505
E-mail: dave2000ad@xc.org
Website: www.harvestprayer.com

Renewal Ministries
3331 Crossfell
Spring, TX 77388
Phone: (281) 355-0269
Fax: (281) 551-8600

Promise Keepers
P.O. Box 103001
Denver, CO 80250-3001
Phone: (303) 964-7600
Fax: (303) 433-1036
Website: www.promisekeepers.org

National Day of Prayer
P.O. Box 15616
Colorado Springs, CO 80935-5616
Phone: (800) 444-8828 or (719) 531-3379
Fax: (719) 548-4520

NATIVE AMERICAN PRAYER

International Reconciliation Coalition for Indigenous People
P.O. Box 1417
Castle Rock, CO 80104
Phone: (303) 660-9258
Fax: (303) 660-0621
E-mail: ircoal@aol.com

NEIGHBORHOOD HOUSES OF PRAYER
LIGHTHOUSES OF PRAYER

Harvest Evangelism
P.O. Box 20310
San Jose, CA95160-0310
Phone: (408) 927-9052
Fax: (408) 927-9830
E-Mail: harvevan@aol.com
Website: www.harvestevan.org

H.O.P.E. Houses of Prayer Everywhere
P.O. Box 141312
Grand Rapids, MI 49514
Phone: (800) 217-5200
Fax: (616) 791-9926
E-mail: hope@missionindia.org
Website: www.missionindia.org/hope

International Renewal Ministries
8435 N.E. Glisan Street
Portland, OR 97220
Phone: (503) 251-6455
Fax: (503) 251-6454
E-Mail: irm@multnomah.edu
Website: www.multnomah.edu

National Pastor's Prayer Network/U.S.
1130 Randville Drive 1D
Palatine, IL 60074
Phone: (847) 991-0153
Fax: (708) 884-9139
E-Mail: phil@nppn.org
Websites: http://www.nppn.org
http://www.missionamerica.org/prayernetwork.html

PRAYER EVANGELISM

Harvest Evangelism
P.O. Box 20310
San Jose, CA95160-0310
Phone: (408) 927-9052
Fax: (408) 927-9830
E-Mail: harvevan@aol.com
Website: www.harvestevan.org

Every Home For Christ
P.O. Box 35930
Colorado Springs, CO 80935-3593
Phone: (719) 260-8888
Fax: (719) 260-7505
E-Mail: info@ehc.org
Website: www.sni.net/ehc

Evelyn Christenson Ministries, Inc.
4265 Brigadoon Drive
St. Paul, MN 55126
Phone: (612) 566-5390
Fax: (612) 566-5390

PRAYER FOR GOVERNMENT LEADERS

Intercessors for America
P.O. Box 4477
Leesburg, VA 20177-8155
Phone: (703) 777-0003
Fax: (703) 777-2324
E-Mail: usapray@aol.com
Website: www.ifa-usapray.org

Lydia Fellowship International
1474 Valcartier Drive
Sunnyvale, CA 94087
Phone: (408) 732-2947
Fax: (408) 732-2972
E-Mail: tryna@bahl.com

PRAYER FOR REVIVAL

Global Harvest Ministries
P.O. Box 63060
Colorado Springs, CO   80962-3060
Phone: (719) 262-9922
Fax: (719) 262-9920
E-Mail: info@globalharvest.org

World Prayer Center
P.O. Box 63060
Colorado Springs, CO 80962-3060
Phone: (719) 536-9100
Email: info@wpccs.org
Website: http://www.wpccs.org

Life Action Ministries
P.O. Box 31
Buchanan, MI 49107
Phone: (616) 684-5905
Fax: (616) 684-0923
E-mail: info@LifeAction.org
Website: www.lifeaction.org

National Prayer Advance
901 E. 78th Street
Minneapolis, MN 55420-1300
Phone: (612) 853-1758
Fax: (612) 853-8488
E-mail: 74114.230@compuserve.com
Website: www.globalharvest.org

YWAM Renewal Ministries
P.O. Box 1634
Port Orchard, WA 98366
Phone: (360) 876-3432
Fax: (360) 876-1332
E-mail: ywamprotorchard@narrows.com
Website: www.ywamprotorchard.com

PRAYER FOR SCHOOLS/TEACHERS

Moms In Touch
P.O. Box 1120
Poway, CA 92074-1120
Phone: (619) 486-4065
Fax: (619) 486-5132
E-mail: mitihqtrs@compuserve.com
Website: www.europa.com/~philhow/moms_in_touch.html

Christian Educators Association Int'l
P.O. Box 41300
Pasadena, CA 91114-8300
Phone: (626) 798-1124
Fax: (626) 798-2346
E-Mail: ceaieduca@aol.com
Website: www.ceai.com

PRAYER NEWSLETTERS & MAGAZINES

MorningStar Journal
16000 Lancaster Hwy.
Charlotte, N.C. 28277-2061
Phone: (704) 542-0278
Fax: (704) 542-0280
Website: www.eaglestar.org

***Pray!* Magazine**
P.O. Box 35008
Colorado Springs, CO 80935
Phone: (800) 263-9240
Fax: (719) 598-7128
E-Mail: pray_mag@navigators.org
Website: www.navpress.org/pray.html

***PrayerNet* Weekly E-mail Newsletter (FREE international)**
SUBSCRIBE: Send a blank email message to
prayernetnewsletter-subscribe@egroups.com
WEBSITE: www.usprayertrack.org

***UpLink* Monthly Postal Newsletter (FREE U.S. only)**
Send your name, address, and phone number to
UpLink, 7710-T Cherry Park Dr., PMB 224, Houston, TX 77095

PRAYERWALKING

Valerie Bell's PrayerWalk Aerobic Cassettes
P.O. Box 1399
Wheaaton, Il 60189
Phone: (630) 668-8412
Fax: (630) 668-8412

WayMakers
P.O. Box 203131
Austin, TX 78720-3131
Phone: (512) 419-PRAY (7729)
Fax: (512) 219-1999
E-Mail: 72650.2666@compuserve.com
Website: www.waymakers.org

RECONCILIATION INITIATIVES

International Reconciliation Coalition
P.O. Box 296
Sunland, CA 91041-0296
Phone: (818) 896-1589
Fax: (818) 896-2077
E-Mail: 75717.777@CompuServe.com
Website: www.reconcile.org

Promise Keepers
P.O. Box 103001
Denver, CO 80250-3001
Phone: (303) 964-7600
Fax: (303) 433-1036
Website: www.promisekeepers.org

SPIRITUAL MAPPING

Sentinel Group
P.O. Box 6334
Lynnwood, WA 98036
Phone: (425) 672-2989
Fax: (425) 672-3028
E-mail: SentinelGp@aol.com
Website: www.sentinelgroup.org

SPIRITUAL WARFARE PRAYER

Frontline Ministries
P.O. Box 786
Corvallis, OR 97339-0786
Phone: (541) 754-1345
Fax: (541) 754-4140
E-Mail: 103112.3123@compuserve.com

Generals of Intercession
P.O. Box 49788
Colorado Springs, CO 80949
Phone: (719) 535-0977
Fax: (719) 535-0884
E-Mail: genint@aol.com

WOMEN'S PRAYER GROUPS

AGLOW International
P.O. Box 1749
Edmonds, WA 98020-1749
Phone: (425) 755-7282
Fax: (425) 778-9615
E-Mail: aglow@aglow.org
Website: www.aglow.org

Prayer Explosion
304 Carriage House Lane
Riverton, NJ 08077
Phone: (609) 786-7233
Fax: (609) 786-1269
E-Mail: oni-prayerexplosion@juno.com

LINC Ministries
P.O. Box 922
Canby, OR 97013
Phone & Fax: (503) 266-9914
E-mail: lincministries@compuserve.com

Reach Out Ministries
3961 Holcomb Br. Rd #200
Norcross, GA 30092
Phone: (770) 441-2247
Fax: (770) 449-7544
E-Mail: 72002.1704@compuserve.com
Website: www.reach-out.org

Appendix B
RECOMMENDED READING

Alves, Elizabeth. *Becoming a Prayer Warrior*. Ventura, CA: Regal Books, 1998.

Anderson, Neil & Charles Mylander. *Setting Your Church Free*. Ventura, CA: Regal Books, 1994.

Bickle, Mike. *Passion for Jesus*. Orlando, FL: Creation House, 1993.

Billheimer, Paul E. *Destined for the Throne*. Ft. Washington, PA: Christian Literature Crusade, 1975.

Bonner, Mickey. *Brokenness, The Forgotten Factor of Prayer*. Houston, TX:
_____*Hearing God's Voice From Within*. Houston, TX:

Cedar, Paul. *A Life of Prayer*. Nashville, TN: Word Publishing, 1998.

Clinton, J. Robert. *The Making of a Leader*. Colorado Springs, CO: NavPress, 1988.

Damazio, Frank. *The Making of a Leader*. Portland, OR: Trilogy Productions, 1988.

_____*Seasons of Intercession*. Portland, OR: BT Publishing, 1998.

Dawson, John. *Healing America's Wounds*. Ventura, CA: Regal Books, 1994.

_____*Taking Our Cities for God*. Lake Mary, FL: Creation House, 1990.

Deere, Jack. *Surprised by the Power of the Spirit*. Grand Rapids, MI: Zondervan Publishing House, 1993.

Eastman, Dick. *The Jericho Hour*. Altamonte Springs, FL: Creation House, 1994.

_____*Love on Its Knees*. Old Tappan, NJ: Fleming H. Revell Co., 1989.

Eckhardt, John. *Moving in the Apostolic*. Ventura, CA: Regal Books, 1998.

Facius, Johannes. *Intercession*. Cambridge, Kent, England: Sovereign World Limited, 1993.

Floyd, Ronnie. *The Power of Prayer and Fasting*. Orange, CA: Sealy Yates, 1997.

Frangipane, Francis. *The House of the Lord*. Lake Mary, Fla.: Creation House, 1991.

Goll, Jim. *The Lost Art of Intercession*. Shippensburg, PA: Revival Press, 1997.

_____*Kneeling on the Promises*. Grand Rapids, MI: Chosen Books, 1999.

Grubb, Norman. *Rees Howells, Intercessor*. Fort Washington, PA: Christian Literature Crusade, 1962.

Guyon, Jeanne. *Experiencing the Depths of Jesus Christ*. Gardiner, ME: Christian Books, 1981.

Haggard, Ted. *Primary Purpose*. Orlando, FL: Creation House, 1995.

Hamon, Bill. *Prophets and Personal Prophecy*. Shippensburg, PA: Destiny Image Publishers, 1987.

Hansen, Jane. *Inside a Woman*. Lynwood, Wash.: Aglow Publications, 1992.

Hawthorne, Steve, and Graham Kendrick. *Prayerwalking*. Orlando, Fla.: Creation House, 1993.

Hayford, Jack. *Built by the Spirit*. Ventura, CA: Regal Books, 1997.

_____*Pastors of Promise*. Ventura, CA: Regal Books, 1997.

Hepner, Ken. *Overcoming Giants of the Heart*. Mukilteo, WA: WinePress Publishing, 1998.

Hinn, Benny. *Welcome, Holy Spirit*. Milton Keynes, England: Word Publishing, 1995.

Jacobs, Cindy. *Possessing the Gates of the Enemy*. Grand Rapids, MI: Chosen Books, 1991.

_____*The Voice of God*. Ventura, CA: Regal Books, 1995.

Jackson, John Paul. *Needless Casualties of War*. Ft. Worth, TX: Streams Publications, 1999.

Jennings, Ben. *The Arena of Prayer*. Orlando, FL: NewLife Publications, 1999.

Kinnamen, Gary. *Overcoming the Dominion of Darkness*. Grand Rapids, MI: Chosen Books, 1990.

Law, Terry. *The Power of Praise and Worship*. Tulsa, OK: Victory House Publishers, 1985.

Murray, Andrew. *The Ministry of Intercession*. Springdale, PA: Whitaker House, 1982.

Marshall, Catherine. *Something More*. New York, NY: Avon Books, 1976.

Mills, Dick. *He Spoke and I Was Strengthened*. San Jacinto, CA: Dick Mills Ministries, 1991.

Mira, Greg. *Victor or Victim*. Grandview, MO: Grace! Publishing Co., 1992.

Murray, Andrew. *The Ministry of Intercession*. Springdale, PA: Whitaker House, 1982.

Nee, Watchman. *Spiritual Authority*. Richmond, VA: Christian Fellowship Publisher, 1972.

_____*The Release of the Spirit*. Cloverdale, IN: Sure Foundation Publishers, 1965.

Otis Jr., George. *The Last of the Giants*. Grand Rapids, MI: Chosen Books, 1991.

_____*Informed Intercession*. Venturay, CA: Regal Books, 1999.

Pierce, Chuck. *Possessing Your Inheritance*. Ventura, CA: Regal Books, 1999.

Prince, Derek. *Shaping History through Prayer and Fasting*. Ft. Lauderdale, FL: Derek Prince Ministries, 1973.

Sandford, John & Paula Sandford. *The Elijah Task*. Tulsa, OK: Victory House, Inc., 1977.

Sapp, Roger. *The Last Apostles on Earth*. Shippensburg, PA: Companion Press, 1995.

Shankle, Randy. *The Merismos*. Marshall, TX: Christian Publishing Services, Inc., 1987.

Sherrer, Quin & Ruthanne Garlock. *A Woman's Guide to Breaking Bondages*. Ann Arbor, MI: Servant Publications, 1994.

_____*The Spiritual Warrior's Prayer Guide*. Ann Arbor, MI: Servant Publications, 1992.

Silvoso, Ed. *That None Should Perish*. Ventura, CA: Regal Books, 1994.

Sjoberg, Kjell. *Winning the Prayer War*. Chichester, England: New Wine Press, 1991.

Smith, Alice. *Beyond the Veil*. Ventura, CA: Regal Books, 1997.

Smith, Eddie. *Help! I'm Married to an Intercessor*. Ventura, CA: Regal Books, 1998.

Smith, Rolland C. *The Watchmen Ministry*. St. Louis: MO: Mission Omega Pub., 1993.

Sorge, Bob. *Dealing with Rejection and the Praise of Man*.

_____*Pain, Perplexity and Promotion*.

Steinbron, Melvin. *The Lay Driven Church*. Ventura, CA: Regal Books, 1997.

Tozer, A.W. *The Knowledge of the Holy*. San Francisco, CA: Harper & Row Pub., 1961.

Wagner, C. Peter. *Breaking Strongholds in Your City*. Ventura, CA: Regal Books, 1993.

_____*Churches That Pray*. Ventura, CA: Regal Books, 1993.

_____*Confronting the Powers*. Ventura, CA: Regal Books, 1996.

_____*Engaging the Enemy*. Ventura, CA: Regal Books, 1991.

_____*Lighting the World*. Ventura, CA: Regal Books, 1995.

_____*Prayer Shield*. Ventura, CA: Regal Books, 1992.

_____*Warfare Prayer*. Ventura, CA: Regal Books, 1992.

_____*Your Spiritual Gifts Can Help Your Church Grow*. Ventura, CA: Regal Books, 1979; Revised Edition, 1994.

White, Tom. *Breaking Strongholds*. Ann Arbor, MI: Servant Publications, 1993.

Appendix C
138 WAYS TO MOBILIZE
PRAYER IN YOUR CHURCH

International:
Praying Through the 10/40 Window
PrayWorld

Nationwide:
National day of prayer
National call to 40-days of prayer and fasting
National Prayer Accord (Churches pray...
Monthly as a church
Quarterly with other churches
Annually as a nation (*PrayUSA!*)
National Native American Day of Prayer
National Day of Prayer for Children
Denominational Leaders' Prayer Summit
Denominational Prayer Leader's Network
Weekly day of fasting and prayer for the nation
National crusade of humility
National concert of prayer
National networks
National day of solemn assembly
Adopting a zip code (or a portion thereof) for prayer

Statewide:
Statewide networks

Countywide:
Prayerwalking every street and road in the county

Citywide:
Citywide networks
Marches for Jesus
Jericho drives
Concerts of Prayer
Prayerwalking
Adopting portions of the city for prayer

Corporate citywide prayer rallies
Human prayer chain around the city
T-shirt chain. (Similar to the above. Each person wears a shirt with one
letter. Standing together beside a street they spell out a Scripture, etc.)

Neighborhood:
Neighborhood houses of prayer
Lighthouses of prayer
Prayerwalking
Door by door prayer ministry

Government Buildings:
Courthouses
City Hall and Court House prayer events
Prisons
Jails

Schools:
Student prayer groups
Student gatherings (See You at the Pole)
Mothers meeting to pray for schools
Teachers meeting to pray at schools
Teachers (privately/personally) prayerwalking their classrooms and campuses
Christians prayerwalking the school campuses (when school is NOT in
session)

Churches:
Watchmen prayer walls
Church staff prayer
Joint corporate prayer for revival among area churches
Korean-style prayer
5 Hours of Power (Corporate prayer, praise, testimonies, Etc.)
(3 hours, 7 hours, etc.)
Concerts of prayer
Prayer rooms
Family prayer
Personal prayer
Prayer chains (telephone, Etc.)
Prayerwalking or drive-by praying to bless them
Intercessory groups to pray for pastors and their families within a city

Groups/Networks:

International
National
Pastors
Children
Youth
Ladies
Mens (Promise Keepers, Etc.)
Student groups
Children's prayer networks
Business groups
Prayer cells
Prayer Triplets
Ladies' prayer cells
Men's prayer cells
Pastors' prayer groups/networks
Pastors' prayer summits
Oil Field Prayer Network, Real Estate or Dentists Prayer Networks, Etc.
Businessmen's & Businesswomen's prayer groups
Professional prayer groups, (Dentists, teachers, Etc.)

Special Times of prayer:

Pre-worship service prayer
Prayer at the 5 Muslim prayer times
Noonday prayer
Mens prayer breakfast
Ladies prayer tea or luncheon
Crisis prayer meetings
Special days of prayer
Lunch-hour prayer fellowship
Early morning, Predawn prayer, Etc.
All-day prayer
24-hour prayer
All-night prayer
First Friday Prayer and Fasting (First Monday, Etc.)

Special Places for prayer:

Prayer journeys
Prayer at spiritual trouble sites, occult centers, etc.
Prayer mountains
Prayer at the high points of the city
Prayer at the cardinal points

Prayer at sea (Revival Cruise)
Prayer in the air (Planes filled with intercessors flying the boundaries of an
    area)
Mobile prayer teams (bicycle, scuba, air, cars, swim, Etc.)
Monthly corporate prayer in city-council chambers

Special Foci:
Prayer/Evangelism
10/40 Window Prayer
Identificational repentance
Prayer on festival days
Jesus Film Project partnership for prayer
Prayer for governmental leaders
Prayer for business and corporate leaders
Prayer for Christian leaders
Prayer for pastors
Chain fasting (one person or church each day)
Prayer for the nations
Prayer for ethno/linguistic people groups
Hospital prayer (Praying for the sick)
Adults adopting children/teens as "prayer parents"
Fasting & Prayer (1, 3, 7, 21 or 40 day, Etc.)
Adopting policemen for prayer "Shield a badge"
Adopting a fireman, a teacher
Adopt a missionary for prayer

Healing the land prayers at massacre sites:
Prayer for persecuted Christians
Doctors praying against abortion
Reconciliation prayer meetings (Racial, gender, denominational, Etc.)
Praying through the phone book
Ramadan Prayer (Praying with and for the Muslim World)
Prayer in mosques, around mosques

Special Training:
Spiritual mapping
Spiritual warfare seminars
Books and booklets
Magazines
Prayer consultations
National prayer centers
Training cassettes and video cassettes

Prayer Conferences
Prayer Seminars
Prayer Retreats
Prayer Banquets

Special Media:
Fax networks
E-mail networks
Telephone prayer chains, prayer hotlines

Radio/Television prayer:
Mailings; prayer letters and bulletins (postal and email)
Building and distributing prayer directories (national, state, city, etc.)

Appendix D
PASTORAL/CHURCH COVENANT FOR PRAYER JOURNEY PARTICIPANTS

A member of your congregation has requested to be a participant in the prayer journey to_____. The participants are being sponsored through churches, personal funds and different parachurch ministries.

As a part of the training and equipping for the prayer journey, we are asking the participants to mobilize local prayer coverage and also send a recommendation from their local pastor or spiritual advisor. The prayer journeys are strategic in nature and it is important that the church cover the participating intercessor in prayer. They will be asking you to please fill out this reference form so we will know they are under authority to a local pastor and church even if a parachurch ministry sends them out.

The U.S. PRAYER TRACK will not be held liable for any accidents, sickness or the death of the participant during the trip. We are requesting that the supporting church commit to provide the intercessor a prayer cover.

PASTORAL REFERENCE FORM:

1. I am aware that _____ is going on a prayer journey to _____ and will covenant to cover him/her in prayer while he/she is on the prayer journey.

2. Years Known: _____

3. Is the character, maturity and life circumstances of the applicant such that you can give a recommendation for participation in a prayer journey?_____ If no, please attach an explanation.

Pastor's Name: _____

Church Name:_____

Church Address: _____

City & State: _____ Zip: _____

Phone: (___) _____ Fax: (___) _____

Email: _____

_____
Pastor's Signature

Appendix E
TEAM COVENANT
FOR PRAYER JOURNEY
PARTICIPANTS

We commit to serve Christ together for a special season of intercessory labor. We desire, personally and corporately, to uphold the following values throughout this endeavor:

* To honor each other, remembering that God has created each of us differently and given each of us differing gifts according to His purpose.

* To bring unity to the team through taking time to be with the Lord to renew ourselves, supporting and ministering to each other, enjoying each other, resolving all personal differences, and forgiving each other as He has forgiven us, so as not to give Satan a foothold.

* To submit to the authority of our leader whom God has appointed over us.

* To strive to be faithful to the task by preparing ourselves spiritually, mentally, and physically; pursuing an attitude of servanthood to the people of _nation_ and to each other, and striving to be faithful servants, as God directs, during this time and in the future.

* To remember that our primary purpose is lost souls and the Kingdom of God. *"The Lord is not slow in keeping His promise, as some understand slowness. He is patient with you, not wanting anyone to perish, but everyone to come to repentance"* 2 Peter 3:9.

Signed: ___/___/2000

Team Member	Signature
1. John Doe	_____
2. _____	_____
3. (Additional lines for each team member's name and signature.)	

• Liability •

I assume all liability for any injury, loss or inconvenience of any incident that may occur while participating in the prayer journey to _____, and therefore won't hold the U.S. PRAYER TRACK, Alice Smith or its staff responsible for incidents that may occur on the trip .

Signed: _____   Date:___/___/2000

*Note: These forms not intended
for legal counsel. Consult with an attorney.*

Appendix F
PERSONAL INFORMATION FORM FOR PRAYER JOURNEY PARTICIPANTS

Date: ___/___/2000   Deadline to return this form: ___/___/2000
Please print your name below, as it will appear on your passport.
NAME: _____
          Last   First   Middle
Informal name: _____
Title: ___ Mr. ___ Mrs. ___ Miss ___ Rev. ___ Dr.
Home Address: _____
City:_____ State: ___ Zip: _____
Home Phone: (___) _____ Work Phone: (___) _____
Occupation: _____SSN#: _____/___/_____Sex: __ M__ F
Country of Citizenship: _____ Passport#:_____
Expiration Date: ___/___/2000

• Family •

1. Marital status: __ Single __ Engaged __ Married __ Divorced __ Separated
2. Spouse's Name: _____
3. Children's names & ages:

_____ ____   _____ ____
_____ ____   _____ ____
_____

• Health/Insurance •

5. Do you consider your health ___ good, ___ average, or ___ poor?
6. Please describe any physical disability: _____
7. Would this problem present physical limitations which might hinder your
involvement in the prayer journey? ___ How? _____
8. Are you currently taking prescription medication? ___ If yes, please explain?
_____
9. Medication allergies?_____
10. Other allergies?_____
11. Do you have health insurance coverage?
Company:_____
Phone: _____ Policy #:_____
12. Will your insurance cover emergencies overseas? _____

• Emergency Contact •

13. Name: _____Relationship: _____
Address: _____
City:_____ State: ___ Zip: _____
Phone: _____
Email: _____

(Continued Next Page)

• Spiritual Background •

14. Briefly describe when and how you came to know Christ personally.
15. How would you describe your relationship with the Lord in the past year?
___ Stagnant ___ Growing ___ Wilderness ___ Learning time ___ Intimate
___ Excellent
16. Describe your involvement in church or parachurch ministry activities in the past.
17. Check any of the following areas you PRESENTLY struggle with or feel the enemy MIGHT have established possible strongholds.
___ Procrastination ___ Laziness ___ Fear(s) ___ Unbelief ___ Lying
___ Prejudice ___ Lust ___ Phobias ___ Rage ___ Control ___ Adultery
___ Rebellion ___ Pornography ___ Moodiness ___ Anxiety___ Chronic fatigue
___ Pride ___ Chronic sickness ___ Critical spirit ___ Self-pity ___ Rejection
___Anger ___ Worthlessness ___ Addictions ___ Jealousy ___ Nightmares
18. Ministry involvement (check areas that apply to you)
         ___ I know how to lead someone to Christ.
         ___ I have been on a deliverance team.
         ___ I have been on a spiritual warfare prayer journey(s):
(where)_____
(when) _____
___ I have been on Mission trip(s):
(where) _____
(when) _____
___ I have been trained in intercessory prayer.
___ I am involved in weekly Bible study or prayer group.
19. Write down your ministry strengths, spiritual gifts or skills, which might be helpful on a prayer journey? (miracles, sing, plays an instrument, discernment, healing, evangelism, mercy)
20. Why do you want to be a part of this prayer journey?
21. Describe your level of experience in the area of warfare prayer. Intercessory prayer? What training have you received?
22. Describe your cross-cultural experience. (traveling overseas into other cultures)
23. What books on prayer have you read recently? (last 5 years)
24. What books on spiritual warfare/mapping have you read recently? (last 5 years)
25. Explain your concept of spiritual warfare. What are your views of demonic strongholds and what authority does the Christian have to displace them?
26. Briefly tell an experience you have had with spiritual warfare. Were you victorious?

• Relational •

27. Do you see yourself as a team player? If no, why not?
28. Explain any difficulties you may have working with other Christians that have doctrinal viewpoints different from your own.
29. Is it difficult for you to follow directions? If yes, explain why.
30. Can you and will you follow the leadership of a woman?_____

(Continued Next Page)

31. You will be expected to travel with the team. There will not be opportunity for individual travel (visiting friends, other ministries, outside tours). Can you accept this policy without reservation? ___Yes ___No

Signature _____ Date _____

Note: These forms not intended for legal counsel. Consult with an attorney.

Conferences, Seminars, Retreats

Eddie and Alice Smith travel worldwide teaching on various themes related to revival and spiritual awakening.

The Smiths teach together as well as separately on topics including prayer, intercession, deliverance, worship, spiritual warfare, spiritual mapping, etc. For information about hosting a conference with the Smiths in your church or city please visit our website at www.usprayertrack.org. Or, send a "blank" email message to request@usprayertrack.org and a "Speaker Invitation Form" will be emailed to you.

Prayer Resources

To order other books and materials by Eddie and Alice, visit our online bookstore at www.usprayertrack.org.

 FREE Newsletters

PrayerNet

Alice Smith is senior editor of this FREE biweekly, informative, up-to-the-minute Internet publication. Join thousands worldwide who receive *PrayerNet*. To subscribe, simply visit our website at www.usprayertrack.org.

UpLink

Subscribe to our FREE monthly postal publication *UpLink* (U.S. addresses only) by calling 713-466-4009 or email your name and address to uplink@usprayertrack.org.

Eddie & Alice Smith
7710-T Cherry Park Drive, PMB 224 • Houston, TX 77095
Phone: (713)466-4009 • Fax: (713) 466-5633
Email: usprayertrack@cs.com
Website: www.usprayertrack.org